# APPROACHES
# TO
# SEMIOTICS

## PAPERBACK SERIES

*edited by*

THOMAS A. SEBEOK

*Research Center for the Language Sciences,*
*Indiana University*

11

# WORDS AND PICTURES

## ON THE LITERAL
## AND THE SYMBOLIC
## IN THE ILLUSTRATION
## OF A TEXT

*by*

MEYER SCHAPIRO

*Columbia University*

1973

MOUTON

THE HAGUE · PARIS

Printed in the Netherlands

# ACKNOWLEDGMENTS

The substance of this book was presented at a symposium, "Language, Symbol, Reality", held at St. Mary's College, Notre Dame, Indiana, on November 7, 1969, and an earlier version in a lecture to the seminar on Hermeneutics at Columbia University in April 1960. For help in the preparation of the book, I wish to thank Dr. Miriam Bunim, and for the index, Dr. Lillian Milgram. For the sources of the illustrations, see the photo credits, page 8.

# TABLE OF CONTENTS

# PHOTO CREDITS

Fig. 1      after E. DeWald, The Utrecht Psalter, n.d., pl. XLb.

Figs. 2, 3, 20      A. de Laborde, La Bible Moralisée, I, 1911, pls. 15, 16, 51.

Fig. 4      J. Wilpert, Die römischen Mosaiken und Malereien der kirchlichen Bauten vom 4. bis 13. Jahrhundert, Freiburg, 1916, pl. 20.

Figs. 5, 6      A. Grabar, The Beginnings of Christian Art, 200-395, New York, 1967, figs. 97, 239.

Fig. 7      M. von Oppenheim, Tell Halaf, n.d. London and New York, pl. VIIIb.

Fig. 8      H. Omont, Miniatures des plus anciens manuscrits grecs de la Bibliothèque Nationale, Paris, 1929, pl. LV.

Fig. 9      W. Neuss, Die katalanische Bibelillustration, 1922, pl. 1.

Fig. 10      A. Goldschmidt, German Book Illumination, New York, 1928, pl. 72.

Fig. 11      P. E. Schramm and F. Mütherich, Denkmale der deutschen Könige und Kaiser, Munich, 1962, pl. 117.

Fig. 12      photo Bibliothèque Nationale, Paris.

Fig. 13      photo British Museum, London.

Fig. 14      Encyclopedia Judaica, Berlin, 1939, vol. 9, frontispiece.

Fig. 15      W. von Hartel and F. Wickhoff, Die Wiener Genesis, Vienna, 1895, pl. XLV.

Fig. 16      Count du Mesnil du Buisson, Les Peintures de la Synagogue de Doura-Europos, Rome, 1939, pl. XXIII.

Figs. 17-19      H. Omont, Psautier de Saint Louis, Reproduction des 92 miniatures du ms. latin 10525 de la Bibliothèque Nationale, Paris, n.d., pls. XXXIV, XXXV, XVI.

Fig. 21      M. Friedländer, Die Lübecker Bibel, Munich, 1923, pl. 25.

Fig. 22      Kunsthistorisches Institut, Universität Marburg, courtesy of Professor Richard Hamann — MacLean.

Fig. 23      Byfield, Holbein Icones, 1830, pl. VIII.

Fig. 24      photo Collection, Columbia University.

Figs. 25, 26      photo Bibliothèque Municipale, Autun.

Fig. 27      photo Richard Hamann, Marburg.

Fig. 27a      A. K. Porter, Romanesque Sculpture of the Pilgrimage Roads, Boston, 1923, ill. 93.

Fig. 28      J. M. Casanovas, C. Dubler, W. Neuss, Sancti Beati a Liebana in Apocalypsin, Codex Gerundensis, Olten and Lausanne, 1962, fol. 257.

Fig. 29      photo Bibliothèque Nationale, Paris.

Fig. 30      photo Max Hirmer, Munich.

Figs. 31, 32      Photo collection, Columbia University.

Figs. 33-35      I. B. Supino, Giotto, Florence 1920, pls. CVIII, CIX, VI.

# 1

# THE ARTIST'S READING OF A TEXT

A great part of visual art in Europe from late antiquity to the 18th century represents subjects taken from a written text. The painter and sculptor had the task of translating the word — religious, historical, or poetic — into a visual image. It is true that many artists did not consult the text but copied an existing illustration either closely or with some change. But for us today the intelligibility of that copy, as of the original, rests finally on its correspondence to a known text through the recognizable forms of the pictured objects and actions signified by the words. The picture, we assume further, corresponds to the concept or memory image associated with the words.

That correspondence of word and picture is often problematic and may be surprisingly vague. In old printed Bibles the same woodcut was used sometimes to illustrate different subjects. These, however, were episodes with a common general meaning. The picture of Jacob's birth was repeated for the birth of Joseph and other scriptural figures, and a battle scene was serviceable for illustrating several such encounters. It is the place of the woodcut in the book, at a certain point in the text, that permits us to grasp the more specific meaning.

Yet in other cases, seeing in a picture only a few elements from a known text, we are able to identify the story. The text is often so much fuller than the illustration that the latter seems a mere token, like a pictorial title; one or two figures and some attribute or accessory object, seen together, will evoke for the instructed viewer the whole chain of actions linked in that text with the few pictured elements, unless an incompatible detail arrests the interpretation. Examples are the paintings in the Christian catacombs of Rome where Noah stands in the ark, Daniel between lions, and Susanna beside the elders. But the meaning of such reductive imagery may be rich in connotations and symbolized values not evident from the basic text itself; these were fixed for the Christian viewer by what he had learned about the same themes from religious commentary and allusions in sermons, ritual, and prayer. Today that fuller meaning has to be recovered through a search of the old writings and contexts; and when we have come to know these, it still remains uncertain which of the various meanings of the subject, embedded in the literary elaborations of the basic text, was intended in a particular labelled image.

Take as an example the episodes from the Old Testament that I have just mentioned. They appear together in prayers in both the synagogue and church as instances of God's intervention to save the faithful in mortal danger. Scholars have explained the choice of those subjects for paintings in the catacombs and for sculptures on sarcophagi as appropriate to the idea of deliverance. But a Greek Christian theologian of the same period, Hippolytus of Rome, interpreted the story of Susanna in another and more complex way in the exegetical style of the time. Susanna, he wrote, is the persecuted church; her husband, Joachim, is Christ; their garden is the society of the saints who are like fruitful trees; Babylon, which surrounds the garden, is the world in which Christians live; the two elders are the two peoples, the Jews and the pagans, who are enemies of the church; Susanna's bath is the water of Baptism that regenerates the church on Easter day; the two maidservants are faith and charity; the perfumes they apply to their mistress' body are the commandments of the Word; and the oil is the grace of the Holy Spirit, especially that which is conferred by confirmation.[1]

Turn now to the catacomb paintings of Susanna and the Elders. We usually see only these three figures on a bare ground; none of the other elements of the story as told in the book of Daniel is represented.[2] In one example Susanna is replaced by a sheep and the elders become two wolves with the inscription *seniores*. The wolves are metaphors that might have a theological sense, for 'wolf' is also a term for heretic. But the wolves are intelligible here through the gospel as figures for evil (Matthew 10:16), and knowing other examples of scenes from the scriptures represented through animal actors, we are satisfied to accept the usual reading of the metaphorical picture as a symbol of deliverance. But we cannot exclude the possibility of other meanings for Christians of that time.

If some illustrations of a text are extreme reductions of a complex narrative — a mere emblem of the story — others enlarge the text, adding details, figures, and a setting not given in the written source. Sometimes the text itself is not specific enough to determine a picture, even in the barest form. Where the book of Genesis tells that Cain killed Abel, one can hardly illustrate the story without showing how the murder was done. But no weapon is mentioned in the text and the artists have to invent the means. Both the Hebrew *vayahargāhu* 'killed him' and its Latin equivalent *interfecit eum* are general terms referring to the effect rather than to the action as such. Yet even the effect here cannot be pictured with both the agent and the victim unless the weapon is shown. Christian folklore and the legends in the Hebrew Midrashim supplied the instrument: a stone, a branch of a tree, a club, a scythe, a jawbone, and still others.[3] Each of these had its ground in the imagined circumstance of the action or even in the name of Cain. It may be a stone because one supposed that the crime was done before there were weapons of iron or bronze; or, remembering that Cain was a farmer, the artist gave him a scythe or hoe. It would seem to follow that the visual image is more concrete than the word; but while this is true in many instances, one can point to verbal accounts with elements of description, physical and psychological, that are not found in the pictures or cannot in principle be translated in all styles of art because of the limited range of their means of representation. In the archaic periods of classic and medieval art painters often felt impelled to inscribe their paintings with the names of the figures and even with phrases identifying the action, although according to a common view, supported by the authority of church fathers, pictures were a mute preaching addressed to the illiterate.

Besides the differences between text and picture arising from the conciseness or generality of the word and from the resources peculiar to verbal and visual art, there are historical factors to consider: (a) the changes in meaning of a text for successive illustrators, though the words remain the same, and (b) the changes in style of representation, which affect the choice of details and their expressive import.

The change of meaning may have different causes. In the pictorial version the original text was often conflated with or contaminated by other texts and images. So in the rendering of the Nativity the familiar and in practice canonical ox and ass have been introduced from a passage of Isaiah (1:3): "The ox knows his owner and the ass his master's crib; but Israel does not know" — a text that perhaps served the Christian polemic against the Jews who would not acknowledge that Christ was the Messiah and thereby forfeited the sense of their Judaic name as the people who know. So too, a fine theological point may determine a detail in the illustration of a text which in itself provides no literal ground for that feature. In pictures of the pentecostal Descent of the Holy Spirit, the Western artists, in accord with the teaching of the Roman church and in opposition to Greek Orthodox doctrine, represent the dove descending from the figure of Jesus Christ as well as from the hand of God the Father — a pictorial statement of the *filioque* that separated the two churches.

For the stylistic factor one may point to the great changes in the imaging of traditional Biblical themes that arose from the norms of Byzantine, Romanesque, Gothic, Renaissance, Mannerist, and Baroque art, each with its own mode of representing action and the setting of a scene. The style as a distinctive habitual system of artistic forms is an expressive vehicle and can modify the often scanty literal sense in the very process of translating the text into an image, especially where the text is the creation of a much older and in some ways more primitive type of art. In each style are rules of representation which, together with the ideas and values paramount in the culture, direct the choice of position, posture, gesture, dress, size, milieu, and other features of the actors and objects.

In giving a pictorial form to figures named in an old text, the painter often represents them anachronistically as people of his own time and place or according to current ideas about the past. No less than the contemporary interests by which the text is colored in the reading, the style of art pervades and remakes what is taken from the text. And with each new style there is a characteristic trend of the imagination in conceiving a subject. The Adoration of the Magi, known through a gospel that does not even number the wise men, is represented at first simply by two, three, or four figures in similar Oriental dress advancing to the seated Mary and child in an undefined space. Later it becomes an elaborate festive scene in a deep landscape with an immense procession of the retinue of three individualized kings and embodies a wealth of allusions acquired through the fantasy of inspired readers and exegetes; written accounts of the story are in turn affected by these paintings. It is such pictorial transmutations of a single text in the course of time that give to iconographic studies their great interest as a revelation of changing ideas and ways of thought.

For Christian readers a text of the Old Testament may have, as I intimated, a symbolic as well as literal sense — symbolic in that the objects and events referred to literally are themselves signs of other objects, actions, and ideas. The symbolic sense, we assume, was usually, if not always, known to the artist. In his illustration of the written word we can sometimes discern effects of the two great trends in Christian Biblical commentary, the one called the Antiochene approach, which explored the literal meaning in order to make it more fully intelligible in terms of the original Jewish context, and the one developed by the early Alexandrian exegetes who looked for a specifically Christian theological, mystical, and moral sense as well, a method that is called the "fourfold interpretation".[4] Much in the Old Testament, taken literally, was obscure, incredible, even scandalous to Christian faith, though it was the word of God; and one had therefore to search for a hidden meaning, deeper and more acceptable, as the pagan Greeks had done with Homer. It should be said that the manifest literal sense, in its fuller detail, is often more than the plain historical fact of an episode in the Jewish past. Reading the account of Abraham's sacrifice of Isaac, we are made aware of an ethical problem and a weighty burden of religious meaning apart from the view of the story as prospectively Christian through the analogy to the sacrifice of Christ.

Another aspect of the illustration of literal meaning is noteworthy in medieval art: the habit of representing the metaphors in the text as if they were simply descriptive terms. When the great artist who illustrated the ninth-century Latin psalter in Utrecht came to the passage in psalm 43 (44): "Awake, why sleepest thou, O Lord", he drew the figure of God lying in bed and awakened by angels (Fig. 1). At the same time this artist introduced in other illustrations of the psalter various episodes from the gospels as allusions manifest to him in the psalmist's words. So for the passage in psalm 86 (87), verse 5: "and of Zion it shall be said, 'This and that man was born in her and the highest himself shall establish her' ", he drew a picture of the birth of Christ.[5] He could have approached psalm 43 (44) in the same allegorizing spirit, like the Byzantine artists who illustrated that verse by alluding to the Resurrection through an apposite image of the Marys at the Tomb.[6] The freedom of interpretation in the Utrecht psalter, with the frequent shift from the literal to the symbolic, while the style of drawing and composition remains the same, is a characteristic feature of this remarkable book.[7]

In certain works the commentator's allegory is made visible through the coupling of the literal illustration with a second picture that represents the symbolic meaning. So at an early period a picture of the Sacrifice of Isaac was paired with a picture of the Crucifixion, and Isaac carrying the Faggots with Christ carrying the Cross. The pages from a Moralized Bible of the 13th century reproduced here are examples of this method (Figs. 2, 3). Yet it must be obvious that even without the concordant image, a picture of Abraham's Sacrifice could be seen as an antetype of the Crucifixion. Sometimes the context, the place of this Old Testament scene in a gospel manuscript or on a cross or altar, would be enough to turn the viewer's mind to Christ. Or this connection could be intimated in a more subtly allusive manner through a single detail: the position of the ram in the bush, suspended by its horns, or the rendering of the bush as a tall plant with two crossed branches, or the faggots on Isaac's shoulders in the form of a cross.[8] But where such pictorial cues were lacking a pious reader was likely to view the literal illustration according to one or another of the different senses expounded by the exegetes and with a focus set by a special interest. For Christians of the early period the Sacrifice of Isaac had been an example of God's help to the soul in danger like Noah in the Flood, Jonah in the whale, Daniel with the lions, and the Hebrew boys in the fiery furnace. It was a promise of salvation through faith and also a model of obedience to God.

But an artist could add a detail or two suggesting ideas that were not part of traditional exegesis and even at times in flagrant deviation from the text. Thus in Souillac in Southern France, on the great sculptured pillar of the 12th century, an angel is shown bringing the ram to the Sacrifice, though the Bible speaks of the ram as appearing miraculously in the bush and orthodox commentary made of this miracle a foreshadowing of Christ on the Cross.[9] The introduction of an angel carrying the ram may be explained by the concern of rationalistic commentators with the question of how the ram got to the site of the Sacrifice — a question already answered by Jewish writers who had speculated on the history of this ram and proposed two alternatives: that the ram was created on the sixth day of the world and kept in heaven for this anticipated occasion, or that it was the bellwether of Abraham's flock, brought by the angel Gabriel.[10] In either case the presence of this detail shows that while theologians were occupied mainly with formal and final causes in explaining the great exemplary events in the Old Testament as prefigurements of the New, others, including artists, were interested as well in the immediate efficient cause of the miracle and applied their fantasy to supply the details of such causation, not provided in the Biblical text. But in Souillac this speculative elaboration of the story has been carried much further. On the other side of the pillar are three superposed scenes of a boy fighting with an old man; in the lowest the boy resists, in the second they struggle, at the top the boy submits; but at that point the victorious old man is himself devoured by a monster. One can interpret the series as a free conversion of the theme of Abraham and Isaac into a struggle between a young man and an old, perhaps son and father — a secular parody with a most serious sense. For a modern observer, schooled in the literature of psychoanalysis, these marginal fantasies are also symbolic as projections of feelings about fathers and sons and transpose to the anonymous secular sphere certain thoughts of resistance and struggle aroused by the story of Abraham and Isaac. But an interpreter who proceeded from the conviction that all imagery in the medieval churches is finally part of a coherent system of religious symbolism would be inclined to see the sculptures of the fighting figures as types of evil, of discord and disobedience, contrasted with the ideal relation of Abraham and Isaac, who in a moment of dreadful anxiety and inner conflict experience a happy deliverance.

# 2

# THEME OF STATE AND THEME OF ACTION (I)

To bring out the interplay of text, commentary, symbolism, and style of representation in the word-bound image, I shall consider at greater length a single text and its varying illustrations. It is Exodus 17:9-13, the story of Moses at the battle with the Amalekites, raising his hands to ensure victory.

9. And Moses said to Joshua: Choose out men for us and go out to fight with Amalek. Tomorrow I will stand on the top of the hill with the rod of God in my hand.
10. So Joshua did as Moses had said to him, and fought with Amalek; and Moses, Aaron, and Hur went up to the top of the hill.
11. And when Moses held up his hand, Israel prevailed; and when he let down his hand, Amalek prevailed.
12. But Moses' hands were heavy. So they took a stone, and put it under him, and he sat on it. And Aaron and Hur stayed up his hands on both sides. And his hands were steady until the going down of the sun.
13. And Joshua discomfited Amalek and his people with the edge of the sword.[11]

For the early Christians this episode was an important antetype of salvation through the cross. It was by assuming the posture of Christ on the cross and making of himself the sign of the cross that Moses overcame Amalek. His general and successor is called Joshua, the Hebrew name of Jesus (Yeshua), which means 'victory'.[12] The author of the epistle of Barnabas[13] and the early apologists, Justin,[14] Tertullian,[15] Origen[16] and Cyprian,[17] all interpreted the story as a foreshadowing of the Cross.[18] It was one of the main examples of their reading of the Old Testament as a prefigurement of the New. A medieval poet, Adam of St. Victor, paraphrasing Hebrews 10:10, expressed the principle concisely:

*Lex est umbra futurorum.* The Old Law is the shadow of things to come. Jewish commentary earlier had found a spiritual symbolism in this story of a battle won through Moses' raised hands: when we look upwards to God, away from earthly things, we prevail; when we look downwards, we are lost.[19] But the prospective method applied by the Church fathers was already clear in the gospels. Speaking to the pilgrims on the way to Emmaus, Jesus, "beginning at Moses and all the prophets, expounded to them in all the scriptures the things concerning himself" (Luke 24:27). Earlier he said to the Jews: "For had ye believed Moses, ye would have believed me, for he wrote of me" (John 5:46, 47); and in foretelling his own death and resurrection he referred to "the sign of the prophet Jonah: 'As Jonah was three days and three nights in the whale's belly, so shall the Son of Man be three days and three nights in the heart of the earth' " (Matthew 12:39, 40).

This reading of the Hebrew Bible as a prefiguration was affirmed by Paul, who saw the crossing of the Red Sea as a baptism and the rock from which Moses brought water for the thirsting Israelites as Christ (I Corinthians 10:1-4). "Now all these things happened to them as examples; and they are written for our admonition upon whom the end of the world is come" (*ibid.*, 10:11).[20]

While an impulse to symbolic interpretation arose in some instances from the need to give to an authoritative but no longer sufficient text a more congenial spiritual sense, the particular prospective symbolism applied here may be traced to Jewish Messianic speculation for which correspondences between past and present, or the past and an awaited future, were signs of a divine plan, a purposive order in history.

The oldest known representation of Moses at the battle with the Amalekites is a mosaic of the fifth century in the nave of Sta. Maria Maggiore in Rome (Fig. 4). Here Moses stands on the hilltop with outstretched hands above the fighting armies. Beside him are Aaron and Hur.

The posture of Moses is like that of many figures in paintings in the catacombs whose gesture has been read as one of prayer; they are called 'orants' and represent supposedly the deceased or a

personification of the pious soul in heaven (Fig. 5). The same
gesture is an attribute of the Old Testament figures already mentioned — Noah, Daniel (Fig. 6), the Hebrew Boys, Susanna —
who are types of faith and deliverance. It has been asked whether
simply prayer is represented by the raised arms, or the sign of the
cross. But for the early Christians there was no ambiguity here
since that posture of prayer with extended arms was regarded as a
sign of the cross.

We note in this first example some differences between image and
text. The artist has chosen the moment when Moses' raised arms
are not yet weary and require no support from Aaron and Hur.
But for this early phase of the battle, the posture is arbitrary with
respect to the written words. These state clearly that Moses carried
a rod, the same rod with which at God's bidding he divided the
Red Sea (Exodus 14:16ff.) and struck the rock in the desert to
bring forth water for his people. God said to Moses: "Go on
before the people, and take with thee of the elders of Israel, and
thy rod, wherewith thou smotest the river, take in thine hand, and
go. Behold, I will stand before thee upon the rock in Horeb, and
thou shalt smite the rock and there shall come water out of it ..."
(Exodus 17:5, 6).[21] In the following account of the battle with the
Amalekites certain of these phrases recur; even the presence of
Aaron and Hur on the hilltop with Moses recalls the elders who
accompanied Moses in the previous action.

The text that the artist had been asked to illustrate was a translation that departs in a significant detail from the Hebrew original.
In the latter and in the Greek, Latin, and English versions, Moses
says that he will stand on the top of the hill and hold the rod of
God in his hand (Exodus 17:9). In the King James translation,
as in the Hebrew text, Moses at first raises a single hand (17:11);
only in the next sentence is there a change to hands in the plural.
But in Jerome's Latin version, as in the Greek Septuagint, both
hands are raised from the start — *cum levaret manus* — and this
reading is followed by the Douay translators.[22] Finally in 17:12
the Hebrew text and all the versions speak of both hands as held
up by Aaron and Hur who have put a stone under Moses for him

to sit on.

Although the shift in the Hebrew text from the singular to the plural of 'hand' seems a contradiction, the plural may be explained as describing the hands raised singly in alternation. When Moses raised one hand and it got tired, he raised the other, and eventually Aaron and Hur sustained both hands while Moses sat on a stone.

Yet one may suppose that the singular of 'hand' in 17:11 refers to the raised hand holding the rod which is the source of Moses' strength and has been effective in dividing the Red Sea (14:16ff.)[23] and in striking water from the rock (17:5-7). In the book of Joshua a similar gesture ensures victory in the battle against Ai. The Lord commanded Joshua: "Stretch out the spear that is in thy hand toward Ai: for I will give it into thy hand. And Joshua stretched out the spear that he had in his hand toward the city. ... Joshua drew not his hand back, wherewith he stretched out the spear, until he had utterly destroyed all the inhabitants of Ai" (Joshua 8:18, 26). In the account of Moses the plural form in the Greek and Latin versions of Exodus 17:11 was perhaps read back by the translators from the next line concerning Aaron's and Hur's support. But in the Hebrew text itself two different symbols of force might have been conflated: the raised hand of a victor, like the hand of God, and the king or god with raised hands supported by his attendants or priests.[24] Both conceptions are found in ancient relief sculptures in the Biblical lands (Fig. 7).[25] The raised right hand is a frequent attribute of power which was transferred from the God of the Hebrew Bible and from images of the pagan divinities and rulers to representations of Christ.[26]

In the Christian world the story of Moses' raised arms was an impressive example of the efficacy of prayer in war and through this sense became a model in actual combat. Many accounts from the Middle Ages tell of a ruler or priest who in the midst of battle remembered this story of Moses and assumed his posture.

Eddi Stephen, the biographer of Bishop Wilfrid of York, reports how during an attack on the Channel coast by pagan enemies in 666 A.D., Wilfrid and his clergy prayed to God. "For as Moses continually called upon the Lord for help, Hur and Aaron raising his hands, while Joshua the son of Nun was fighting against Amalek with the people of God, so this little band of Christians overthrew the fierce and untamed heathen host."[27]

In Ireland where the action of Moses was a constant theme and one likened the national saint, Patrick, to the Jewish leader, there was practiced a type of ascetic prayer, the cross-vigil, in which the monk or hermit held his arms up for long periods in imitation of Moses on the hill. This mode of prayer was ascribed to saints Columba (Columcille) and Finnian during a battle between two rival Irish armies over possession of a copy of Columba's famous psalter; each saint, like Moses, kept his arms raised in prayer for the victory of his own side.[28]

In 796 Charlemagne wrote to Pope Leo III that while it was the king's task to support the church by arms, "your task, very holy father, consists in seconding the success of our arms by raising your hands to God, like Moses, and imploring him to give the Christian people victory over the enemy of his name".[29]

In the next Germanic dynasty in the tenth century, the emperor Otto I in battle "remembered how the Lord's people had overcome the Amalekites' attack through the prayers of Moses, the servant of God. Accordingly he leaped down from his horse and burst into tearful prayers", kneeling before the nails of the Cross which were fixed on a miracle-working spear.[30]

A little later, around the year 1000, King Robert of France is described by his biographer, Helgaud, as serving God and triumphing over his enemies by virtue of the Holy Spirit, just as Moses, the servant of God, won a victory over Amalek by praying humbly with his arms outstretched.[31]

In the first crusade the animating role of the Church inspired what may be taken as the classic statement of this likeness of contemporary and Biblical wars. Pope Urban in his speech at Clermont in 1095 proclaimed to the soldiers: "You who are to go shall have us praying for you; we shall have you fighting for God's people. It is our duty to pray, yours to fight against the Amalekites. With Moses we shall extend unwearied hands in prayer to heaven, while you go forth and brandish the sword, like dauntless warriors, against Amalek."[32]

In these accounts it is sometimes a priest who reenacts the role of Moses, sometimes a king. Yet few of the texts allude to the symbolism of the cross in Moses' posture of prayer, though the extension of the arms is cited. The literal sense of the few words in the Bible — literal as understood by the men of the Middle Ages — was enough ground for their application to a present combat in which prayer could bring victory. And even apart from the connection with prayer, the raised arm had its own magical and poetic force as 'the upper hand' in a battle.

By the time of Pope Urban's speech the picture of the episode had changed in an important respect. From the ninth century onward we see the arms of Moses held up by Aaron and Hur. The oldest example of this type, preserved in a Greek manuscript of the Homilies of Gregory Nazianzen, dated about 880, probably goes back to an earlier model (Fig. 8).[33] The same conception appears in illustrated Greek Octateuchs of the 11th and 12th centuries which depend on a much older prototype.[34] But no examples of the subject have survived from the mid-fifth to the ninth century, and we are unable to say just when the new type was introduced. In the Gregory manuscript the image of Moses, Aaron, and Hur illustrates an allusion to the episode in a sermon that speaks of Moses alone, unaided by his two companions.[35] In the West we find the same motif of the two men sustaining Moses' arms in a Bible of 960 in León (fol. 40v), and in the following century in two separate drawings in the Catalonian Bible of Farfa (Fig. 9),[36] and a third in Aelfric's Paraphrase of Exodus in the British Museum.[37] In the latter and in the second of the drawings in the Farfa manuscript we note another feature newly selected from the text: the position of Moses sitting on a stone when Aaron and Hur support his hands (Exodus 17:12). This stone was not just a seat for his weary body, added in a spirit of realism, but was perhaps understood in the Middle Ages as a seat of honor, a throne, that served as a sign of his theocratic power.[38] In the Vulgate, a few lines beyond (17:16), Moses recalls God's promise that he will destroy Amalek "by the hand of the throne of the

Lord".[39]

There is in Western art since the 11th century, with the emergence of the so-called Romanesque style, a notable trend to fuller illustration of a narrative text. But the motif of the supported arms precedes that trend; and occurring as it does in both Byzantine and Western art, it also invites the question of possible dependence in the West on Greek examples — though, given the common text, an independent choice of the same detail is conceivable in West and East. One can readily imagine that a reader of the text, inclined to the dramatic in the narrative, was impressed by the second stage of the battle, when the leader's arms became weary and had to be held up by others. As a turn of fortune and its reversal through a new action, this moment of the story has an evident appeal and might have inspired the variant image without a prompting of the artist by an ideological interest. I have made the experiment of reading the text to two children aged nine and seven, whom I asked then to draw a picture of the action. Both showed Moses supported; but while the younger represented the two helpers sustaining Moses' arms together, the older boy had only one hold up an arm of Moses while the second stood by inactive. Perhaps he wished the role of supporter for himself alone or, identifying himself with Moses, he imagined a single support — his brother.

I do not believe that in the Middle Ages a traditional picture rendering a sacred text could be changed so readily after a fresh scrutiny of the words. What we wish to understand is the creation of a new type that was widely accepted and replaced an older standard image. If in a modern child's attraction by the idea of the supported arms there may be a psychological pattern arising from needs of the child within the context of his family life and the enjoyment of an imagined role through the story, a corresponding concept latent in a medieval artist had to contend with the authority of an existing model. Yet we know from the history of many such images that compulsion by the model is not so strong as to preclude individual revisions which are then maintained by a new common interest or viewpoint.

For the character of the earliest image of the story, known through the unique example in Sta. Maria Maggiore, I venture the following explanation of its disregard of those features of the text that seem to us so obviously dramatic. Moses as a hero was represented there according to the norm of contemporary classic art which supplied the first Christian painters and sculptors with models. A victorious hero then was generally an isolated statuesque figure even in a group composition. To attach to him two other standing figures as supports would have lessened his distinct self-sufficient being. And this classic conception of the hero was all the more appropriate in a Christian art devoted to a symbolic imagery of divine aid; it was not the physical support by Aaron and Hur but God's intervention through Moses that brought victory.

If we look for a conception favorable to that image of a support in a medieval context, we shall find it precisely in a field that has some similarity to the story of Moses, Aaron, and Hur in the battle.

In two pictures of the German king Henry II (1002-14), one in a sacramentary and the other in a pontifical, he is shown with raised arms supported by two native saints in episcopal dress. In the first (Fig. 10) Henry receives his crown from Christ above him and two angels hand him the other insignia of power — the lance and the sword. It is a scene of investiture symbolizing the sacred authority of the ruler. A punning inscription refers to Henry as Christ's anointed *(xpictos)*.[40] In the second manuscript the heavenly figures are lacking (Fig. 11), but there is the same analogy of the king to Christ through his posture as a cross and to Moses through the supporting bishop-saints.[41] That was how the ruler was conducted into the church on certain feast days and at his coronation.[42]

One may suspect in the likening of Henry to Moses an emulation of the Byzantine monarch, the rival claimant of the Roman imperial crown. Since the time of Constantine the East Roman ruler had been called a second or new Moses. Constantine's victory over Maxentius at the Milvian bridge was compared by his biographer to the victory of Moses over Pharaoh at the Red Sea; and the miraculous rod through which the Jewish leader had prevailed was preserved in the Byzantine capital in a chapel of the palace and carried as an insigne in imperial ceremonies and processions.[43]

If in the image of Christ crowning the Byzantine emperor, which was the model of the crowning of the Western ruler, the Greek autocrat's arms are not held up by bishop-saints who stand beside him, it may be that his old authority as a 'universal bishop' in the Greek church did not admit so explicit a sign of dependence. In the Venice psalter of Basil II (976-1025), in the frontispiece showing his consecration by Christ and angels, he stands above eight prostrate figures and is flanked by armed warrior saints who are invoked in battle.[44] In a traditional ceremony the new Byzantine ruler was elevated on a shield by his soldiers, a rite of pagan German and late Roman origin which is represented in Byzantine psalters as an episode in the crowning of David.[45]

In the West the likeness of the ruler to Moses had been spelled out in the eighth century. When Pope Stephen II in 754 found it expedient to invest the Frankish king, Pippin, with a sacred authority through the Old Testament rite of anointing, as a helpful ally and counterforce in checking the advance of the Lombard king in the papal states, he addressed Pippin as a "new Moses and a new David".[46] In 747 Pope Zacharias had written Pippin that just as Moses prayed while Joshua triumphed in battle, so should the Franks fight while the clergy supported him by prayer and counsel.[47] The authority of Pippin, who, having displaced the legitimate but weak Merovingian ruler, could not claim a hereditary kingship, was strengthened by the sacramental anointing. He was the first Frankish ruler to be consecrated like an Old Testament king; and the papacy in supporting him in this way recalled the precedent of Samuel dethroning Saul and choosing David.

In these letters and ceremonies, as in the texts cited above, the role of Moses is ascribed at one point to the ruler and at another to the priest. Both are at the same time religious and secular powers in close alliance with each other, an alliance founded on mutual dependence and often disrupted in the following centuries by a conflict of interest. If the image of the archetype priest Aaron, together with his brother-in-law Hur, supporting the arms of Moses in battle could appeal to both the Greek and Latin churches, its counterpart in the picture of the ruler is known only in the West.

The sacredness of the Byzantine emperor and his power in the Greek church were not subject to the same challenges and strains as the authority of the German emperor in the Roman Church which, while calling on his support, often resisted his claims. It is hard to imagine in Byzantium the complementary symbol of the rulers sustaining the church, as represented in a drawing of the 11th century from Echternach with the crowned Mary-Ecclesia enthroned between the kings David and Solomon who support her raised arms (Fig. 12).[48]

The image of a royal or sacred personage with arms held up by other figures may be a sign of power apart from these special relations of medieval priest and king. It may express not a dependence of the supported figure but his power to command support. The scheme of the raised arms, with or without supporting figures, is, I have said, an ancient one in the pre-classic world of the Hittites and Babylonians.[49] It is a widespread form known also in the old African kingdom of Benin where many bronze images have been found of a ruler with raised arms held up by two smaller attendants.[50] Supporting figures in other contexts make visible the majesty of Christ and the power of a bishop. Christ sits or stands in a mandorla held up by two or four angels; sometimes he is shown being lifted up more directly by angels in his Ascension.[51] On a throne in Bari small crouching figures support the bishop's seat.[52]

This old conception of a supported power survived into Italian Renaissance art. Representing Ezekiel's vision of the tetramorph, Raphael placed God in heaven with raised arms held up by two angels. I do not know through what channels Raphael received this extraordinary image. It is not founded on Ezekiel's text.[53]

# 3

# THEME OF STATE AND THEME OF ACTION (II)

If there is a doubt that in the Middle Ages one saw in Moses' raised arms a prefigurement of the cross — since the analogy is often not explicit in the pictures and the texts — one can point to a negative evidence of this reading of the scene. It is a miniature in a Hebrew manuscript produced in Paris about 1278 (Fig. 13).[54] Here Moses holds both hands close to his breast, a common posture of prayer in Christian art as well. The painter might have been a Christian of the Paris school of miniaturists; but we would suppose then that he followed here the instructions of a Jewish owner of the book. The Hebrew inscription below says that when Moses raised his *hand (yado)*, the Israelites prevailed. The illustration of the story, while in accord with the Christian choice of Aaron and Hur — though the battle itself is ignored — was apparently designed to avoid the repugnant symbolism of the outstretched hands. The seated position of Moses on the stone is perhaps an expression of Jewish reverence of the leader. But other miniatures in the same manuscript, e.g., the Sacrifice of Isaac, are indistinguishable from examples in Christian painting that follow the literal text and are probably patterned on these models.

The arms raised outwards do occur, however, in another Jewish manuscript, a work of the sixteenth century, in the Berlin Library (Fig. 14).[55] But this miniature, which might have been based on a Christian work, was done in Persia in a Moslem milieu where the symbolism of the cross was not as disturbing a factor for a Jewish reader of the book.

Students of Jewish commentaries on the Old Testament have noted that certain themes were reinterpreted by the rabbis to preclude a Christian interpretation. During the first centuries A.D., when the apologists of the new religion spoke of their sect as the 'true Israel' *(verus Israel)* and polemicized against Judaism as ignorant and obsolete, the rabbis restated in self-defense the meaning of certain words and episodes of their Bible that were being cited as prophecies and prefigurements of Christ.[56] This process may be observed also in art.

A favored text in Christian polemic against the Jews was chapter 48:13-19 of Genesis describing Jacob's blessing of the sons of Joseph.[57] Joseph placed Manasse, the older son, at Jacob's right hand, and the younger Ephraim at the left; but Jacob crossed his hands in order to give the greater blessing to Ephraim in spite of Joseph's protest. Christian writers found in this episode a prefigurement of the cross, a meaning reinforced by Jacob's preference for the younger son, Ephraim; the Old Law was replaced by the New, and Ephraim as the ancestor of the Messiah in Jewish belief, pointed to Christ. In a Greek manuscript of Genesis in Vienna, Jacob's blessing is illustrated by a scene of ritual formality with a prominent crossing of hands (Fig. 15). But in a painting of the same subject in the Dura synagogue (ca. 245 A.D.) the crossing is ignored (Fig. 16).[58]

This reflex of inhibitory interpretation to avoid a distasteful analogy may be found also in Christian art. When illustrating the episode of the hanging of the king of Ai, described in the book of Joshua (8:29), Byzantine artists chose to represent the cross-pattern of the twin-beamed gallows *(epi xylou didymou)* as a stake or *furca* and showed the victim in profile.[59] Pagan opponents of Christianity had mocked the cult of a God crucified like a common criminal. Constantine after his conversion abolished the cross as an instrument of punishment, replacing it by the forked stake.[60] In Jerome's translation of the book of Joshua there still appears the word '*crux*' (8:29);[61] but Western artists avoid the literal rendering and represent a one-armed gallows,[62] even in the rare instance where the deposition of the king's corpse is likened to the deposition of Christ.[63]

For the reader who has followed the account to this point and kept in mind the analogy of Moses to Christ, it will be a surprise to see the miniature painting of our scene in a psalter of Louis IX (Paris, Bibliothèque nationale, ms. lat. 10525), contemporary with the Jewish example (Fig. 17). Here Moses appears in profile kneeling, with hands close together, a posture that is as far from the pattern of the cross as one can imagine. Has the artist deliberately turned away from the symbolism and ignored the long tradition of church commentators? Elsewhere in the book he has represented other praying figures — Samson, David, and Moses at the burning bush — in the same realistic manner, kneeling and in profile.[64] It seems that another pictorial sign for prayer has been applied to Moses, replacing the sign that had been standard in early Christian art and had served to make more evident the symbolism of the cross in this scene.

The change from the frontal to the profile position of Moses may be explained by a characteristic of the art of that time: the heightened interest in action, whether in religious or secular scenes, as an objective engagement in which the actors move in a common space of their own and are attentive to each other without confronting the viewer of the image as in a theme of state.

Represented as in the same field with the fighters and turned towards them, Moses appears to take part in the battle. His arms extend towards the soldiers like weapons in the actual combat, and he kneels as in ordinary prayer.

In the older images of Moses his frontal posture and his position between Aaron and Hur isolate him from the battle, in accord with the text which places him on the hilltop, and give him the character of a sacred person in his own higher sphere of being. In the early Christian and Byzantine examples he recalls the emperor in certain official representations, enthroned ceremonially above a zone of smaller profile figures in homage, games, or combat.

Though the artist of the psalter favors the profile — whether a strict or a near-profile — as more suited to action, he has not given up entirely the frontal pose with raised hands. But in a remarkable picture where he does use it — the scene of Joseph disclosing himself to his brothers — this posture too belongs to action (Fig. 18). In a subtle way it is both acting in the theatrical sense and an act of self-revelation. Joseph throws off his robes of office and stands up, raising his arms high. Doing so, he recalls to the others his posture when they had last known him as their brother — earlier in the same book the artist represented Joseph being lowered into the well, with his arms raised high (Fig. 19). There is in this climactic pose a reminder of Christ on the cross; indeed Joseph betrayed by his brothers and then saving them in Egypt was a striking figure of Christ for the early Church writers as later for Pascal.[65] But the power of the image (Fig. 18) lies rather, I think, in the shock of revelation. The moment of disclosure — a poignant evocation of a past that also foreshadows the Christian future — has been realized through a brilliantly conceived form in which self-reference, remembering, and fateful action are condensed in a single dramatic posture.

From the shift to the profile in the picture of Moses at the battle it does not follow that the old symbolic meaning had disappeared altogether. In the 13th century many viewers of this profile image of Moses, with arms held up by Aaron and Hur, might still recall the Christian sense of the episode, just as a picture of Abraham's Sacrifice could awaken an idea of the crucifixion though the picture contained no element patterned like the cross.

But there is reason to think that by this time the symbolic sense of Moses' prayer had indeed changed. In the illustration of the scene in the Moralized Bible of ca. 1245 (Fig. 20) a new meaning is made as explicit as one could wish.

Before I describe the miniature I should like to say more about the character of this extraordinary volume.[66] It is an immense picture book where each historical scene of the Old Testament is accompanied by a second picture that conveys the symbolic meaning of the first (Figs. 2, 3). While ordinarily the pictures in a Bible illustrate the preexisting text, here the written text consists of short inscriptions that describe the paired pictures and explain their connection. These pictures are images of two distinct events or situations, which in turn are understood as the symbol and the symbolized. Although this ordered collection of pictures may be likened to a dictionary where each word is coupled with a defining phrase or with a synonym, the principle of the picture Bible is different. The two images are not substitutable for each other; they are analogous rather than equivalent and the events they depict have an irreversible relation in time. Their analogy points to a divine intention that has determined the two pictured events and their historical connection — a complex causal tie. The first is a sign and preparation of what is to come, as a dark cloud is a sign of rain; but in the scriptural sphere the unique portending events are signs only to a believing reader who knows the unfolding plan of history in which both the portent and its completion issue from God's will.

In the Moralized Bible a scene of ritual follows the picture of Moses: a priest prays at the altar, while figures of God the Father and Christ support his raised hands; with them is a dove representing the Holy Spirit; behind the priest are the laity, all with arms lifted in prayer and all treading on demons.

The inscription of the upper medallion says: "When Moses raised his hands, Israel conquered; when he lowered them a little, Amalek prevailed." The text explaining the second scene reads: "Moses who lifts up his hands which Aaron and Hur support while he prays so that God may give victory signifies the prelate who lifts up his hands high at the sacrament of the altar; the Father and Son support him and the Holy Spirit sends him the body of the Son by whose presence victory is given to God's people and the vices are defeated."

The sense of the story of Moses has changed from a prefigurement of the Cross to a fore-symbol of the priest at the altar. To be sure, the priest is himself a figure of Christ when he performs the sacrifice of the Mass. But new here is the specific content of the symbolism of the first scene. A historical episode of the Old Testament signifies now a commonly experienced contemporary event, a recurrent rite, though the artist does not find it inconsistent with this visible actuality of the rite to include in his picture the invisible divine beings named in the words of the Mass and to represent literally as a physical act the metaphor of spiritual support, perhaps to affirm the doctrine of the real presence. The victory over Amalek is likened then to the victory of souls fortified by the sacrament in their perpetual struggle against sin.

From the prevailing system of scriptural interpretation the author of the Moralized Bible has selected as the essential meaning of the Moses story a liturgical and moral symbolism; but the artist in representing Moses has held to the older analogy to Christ on the Cross.

This pictorial conception of the Biblical episode, with Moses compared to Christ and the whole serving as a symbol of the Sacrifice of the Mass, was perhaps based on an earlier illustration. It had already been expressed in the 12th century by Honorius, an author widely read in his time. Explaining the office of the Mass, he wrote:

In it are represented the sacrifice of the highest pontiff (sc. Christ) and the battle of the King of Glory. Moses prefigured it when he prayed on the mountain with outstretched hands, while Joshua, who is Jesus, fought with Amalek, devastated the kingdom of the defeated enemy, and brought back his people joyous in victory. Thus Christ on the mount of the Cross prayed with outstretched hands for the unbelieving and denying people and, as a victorious leader *(dux)*, fought under the standard of the Cross against Amalek, that is, the devil, and laid waste his conquered kingdom; having defeated the evil enemy, the Lord despoiled Hell.

... Mystery. The bishop images all this and tries to express it in dramatic dress. When he recites the canon with outstretched hands, he represents Christ nailed on the Cross as if he is fighting Amalek, while he simulates Christ's struggle against the devil with the signs of the crosses. Moreover the priests are stationed like the sharp weapons of the fighters, while the deacons are placed behind the bishop and the subdeacons behind the altar.[67]

Note in the Moralized Bible that while the historic priestly group — the praying Moses with Aaron and Hur — is presented as if turned to the viewer in a broadly frontal centralized design and the fighting soldiers below cluster and cross in varied positions ranging from full-face to three-quarters to profile, the medieval priest and his spiritual supports are aligned all in near-profile, as in many pictures of a real church ceremony in that period. The unique frontality and symmetry of Moses is an artistic mode of presenting a transcendent figure or sacred theme of state; the repeated profile of the symbolized content is that of an ongoing action of which the ordered ritual character is marked by its difference from the spontaneity and chaos of the battle. Full-face and profile, though less strict than in some earlier works, function here as contrasted forms of the symbol and the symbolized. Even God the Father and Christ, who are so often shown frontally to convey their sacred unconditioned being, appear in the same empirical profile as the worshippers and the priest. The text of Honorius speaks three times of the outstretched hands of Moses, Christ, and the bishop as a pattern of the cross; but in the Moralized Bible the empirical mode of representation is stronger than the word and in the picture of the symbolized action the artist has replaced the significant symbolic posture by the less evocative profile of figures in a transient action. And one will observe that even in the upper medallion Moses' figure is less pronounced as a cross than in some older images.

We have seen that in the 13th century, not long after the Moralized Bible was made, another French artist, representing the story of Moses by itself without indicating the symbolic sense through metaphoric detail or an accompanying explanatory miniature or inscription, drew Moses in profile. Here the analogy to the cross may be implied but is not manifest. The symbolic content of the episode was no longer expressed in the form of the represented posture.

Was the shift to the profile in that picture of Moses a deliberate detheologizing of the story? If the frontal form with its symmetrical cross pattern brought out the Christian sense by analogy, did the profile by contrast convey an idea of the historic event in its concrete actuality? Or, without ascribing to the artist so definite an aim in a particular work, was the change from the frontal to the profile Moses an instance of a more general change from the providential Christian view to the plainly empirical in the imaging of historical scenes of the Old Testament that had once been grasped as symbols of the New?

From later pictures it is clear that the role of Moses at the battle had come to be seen as a minor detail of the action, though perhaps retaining its Christian connotation for some viewers. In a woodcut in the Lübeck Bible of 1494 Moses kneels and prays in profile, while Aaron and Hur support his arms; the three are at the side of the picture while the battling armies fill the greater part of the space (Fig. 21).[68] This is how the scene is often represented in Bibles of the 17th century as well.[69] Sometimes the praying group is set far off in the landscape and diminished in size by the perspective.[70]

An exceptional image of about 1300 on a decorated tile from the pavement of St. Nicaise in Reims shows how far one had moved from a symbolic rendering of the story (Fig. 22).[71] Moses appears with his left arm raised; his two companions help to support it. The artist, we may suppose, had responded to the Hebrew text which tells of Moses raising a single arm. Here the newly marked literal detail is a significant selection; one chose the hitherto ignored moment in which the leader's raised arm works as a magic force like Jehovah's 'mighty hand'.[72]

How much the symbolism of the cross in this scene had declined in importance we may judge also from an illustration of the battle in a magnificent royal picture book of the Old Testament produced in Paris about 1250 and now in the Morgan Library. It is one of the fullest series of such pictures, yet the battle of Joshua's army and the Amalekites is represented there without Moses.[73] The painter's chief interest is in the world of combat; the Old Testament is for him a secular history with memorable tales of war, adventure, and love.

Throughout the Middle Ages the narrative books of the Old Testament had been read from a lay point of view as an epic of Jewish heroes and heroines, ideal in courage, wisdom, and beauty. Joshua, Gideon, Samson, Solomon, Judith, and others were often named in courtly literature as noble types beside those of the Greek and Roman world. For feudal imagination the Old Testament had a legendary, even pagan, aspect and its kings were the models of a heroic royalty for which the Gospels could provide no precedent. Episodes of the Jewish Bible were quoted then as history and poetic example without regard to the fourfold interpretation.

As with the story of Moses, the secularizing trend in the illustration of a Biblical narrative text, very strong in the late Middle Ages, may be traced also in pictures of Jacob Blessing the Sons of Joseph. By the 16th century this episode, which for medieval religious thought was so highly charged with allusions to Christ and the Church, could be represented in complete abstraction from orthodox commentary. I show a woodcut from a Latin Bible published in Paris in 1560 (after a woodcut by Holbein) where neither the crossing of Jacob's hands nor the choice of the younger son for the primary blessing has been rendered, although these details are explicit in the text (Fig. 23).[74]

Even Rembrandt, a deeper artist who was a close reader of the Bible and surely grasped the spiritual complexity of the story, ignored the Christian sense in his painting of the subject (Fig. 24). Placing the emotional content, the grandfather's tender love of the child, above theology and the physical details of the rite, he omitted the crossing of the hands; only one hand is clearly shown and its gesture of blessing is in profile.

As more naturalistic styles prevailed in art, the prefigurative interpretations of a narrative, transmitted by the later exegetes, became less cogent, though they retained their appeal in liturgical contents and in didactic art. The religious too sometimes spoke of them as curiosities of an affected, outmoded reading of the sacred book. One could excuse them as a kind of poetizing, a search for analogies pleasing to the imagination; but they were hardly satisfying to common sense or reason when presented as insights into a divine plan underlying the historical events.

Early in the 13th century a philosopher-theologian and archbishop of Paris, William of Auvergne, questioned the practice of interpreting the Old Testament as a prefigurement of the New. He accepted the analogies as descriptive or metaphorical, not explanatory. An expositor could make use of one event as a simile to describe another which it resembled in form; but the resemblance did not signify a connection of cause or purpose between the two events.[75]

It is as such a poetic analogy that the story of Moses, Aaron, and

Hur has reappeared in our own time, and in a most unlikely place. The biologist, Peter B. Medawar, writing on logical syntax and semantics in a "Note on Scientific Method" in his book, *The Uniqueness of the Individual*, says: "A scientific theory is propped up on either side, like Moses' arms before the Amalekites, by twin supports that together form its 'metatheory', and without these Reason cannot prevail."[76]

# 4

# FRONTAL AND PROFILE AS SYMBOLIC FORMS

I shall discuss further in this last part the role of the style of representation in the form of the symbol, and more specifically the frontal and profile positions.

Meaning and artistic form are not easily separated in representations; some forms that appear to be conventions of a local or period style are not only aesthetic choices but are perceived as attributes of the represented objects. What is called frontality may be one of several natural appearances favored in a given style, all rendered with the same kind of line and modelling; or it may be a dominant and even exclusive posture, applied to figures with different meaning, and by its distinctive qualities and accord with other features of the work it may stand out as a pronounced characteristic of the style. The same alternatives hold for the profile position.

The frontality, symmetry, and central place of Moses in some of our examples belong to life as well as art. We know them as features of ritual, a domain of the real in which every detail is a sign. Once they have been established, the dramatic and voiced forms of liturgy created for invocation and reminder of the sacred undergo little change, while furniture, vessels, and vestments are continually redesigned to satisfy a new taste in art. But pictures of the same ritual vary from age to age and show the influence of a style of art. In a style committed to a clear view of the figures in a scene, with little or no spatial depth, the painter will not show a rite in perspective as beheld from the nave. He is more likely to represent priest and worshippers aligned in profile.[77] Yet the same artist, to exhibit the clergy as a hierarchy, will choose another arrangement more suited to the expression of rank. An instructive example of the different approaches are two miniatures in the Sacramentary of Marmoutier, a Carolingian manuscript of the school of Tours (Figs. 25, 26). In the scene of the abbot Raganaldus blessing the monks and laity, all the figures, including the abbot, are in profile; but in the picture representing the hierarchy from bishop to acolyte the differences of rank are made visible through differences of position with respect to the center and through elevation, size, posture, and glance — ranging from the seated bishop, strictly frontal in the center, to the profiles of the lowest and outermost figures.[78]

In medieval art basically different modes of composition coexist within the same personal or collective style, adapted to different types of content, like the modes in music and the genres in poetry. Elements of two such modes may be used within a single image to convey a duality of meanings or to mark an important distinction.

The effects of profile and frontal depend also on their relation to another prevalent type. Since late antiquity and throughout the Middle Ages a schematized three-quarters face was a standard form. It combined aspects of the full-face and profile, independent of an explicit connection of the eye or hand with a specific object. This generalized posture of the head — a vestige of an advanced naturalistic model inherited from classic art — satisfied the archaic need for distinctness and completeness by showing both eyes clearly and the nose in its characteristic profile, while retaining a suggestion of movement. The dominance of the three-quarters view gave to the exceptional profile or frontal figure the value of the unique or the opposed.

In many pictures of the frontal figure the head is turned slightly; the nature of the contrast of frontal and profile as different relations of a subject to an observer will be most evident through comparison of the profile with the strict full-face as an extreme position. The profile face is detached from the viewer and belongs with the body in action (or in an intransitive state) in a space shared with other profiles on the surface of the image. It is, broadly speaking, like the grammatical form of the third person, the impersonal 'he' or 'she' with its concordantly inflected verb; while the face turned outwards is credited with intentness, a latent or potential glance directed to the observer, and corresponds to the role of 'I' in speech, with its complementary 'you'. It seems to exist both for us and for itself in a space virtually continuous with our own, and is therefore appropriate to the figure as symbol or as carrier of a message. That a figure of Christ holding a book inscribed *Ego sum lux mundi* should be drawn full-face is obvious and natural, since it is addressing the viewer. Yet even when representing a particular individual, whether divine or human, the full-face form, especially of the free-standing, isolated sculpture in the round and of the painted or relief image well above the viewer's eye-level, may be of the generalized, the abstract man, outside any context and without the subjectivity implied in a glance. In such figures the eyes are often without a pupil and have been interpreted as expressions of a stage in cultural development before thought had reached a truly reflective self-awareness. The eye without sign of attentiveness seems inactive then like the body as a whole.

Yet we are inclined to see whatever faces us as looking at us, particularly if the image is isolated or in the center of its field, even though the eyes are unmarked by iris and pupil. The frontal eyes in a head represented full-face, on or near our own eye-level, hold our gaze and seem to follow us as we move to left or right. This uncanny appearance of the frontal head is the source of medieval texts that speak of an image as miraculously observant and addressing the viewer, or take it as a model of the ubiquitous, all-seeing God.[79] Baudelaire who knew the sensational recent discoveries of the ancient Oriental temples with their giant sculptures saw these as symbolic figures that speak to us and penetrate us with their intimate glance:

> La nature est un temple où de vivants piliers
> Laissent parfois sortir de confuses paroles;
> L'homme y passe à travers des forêts de symboles
> Qui l'observent avec des regards familiers.[80]

Besides these qualities of the full-face and profile in art, grounded in the everyday experience of the human presence, one must take into account in the choice of these views and their pairing the artist's requirement of balance, contrast, accent, and variation. The exceptional frontal head in a large series of profiles may be unmarked by other traits that singularize that figure as specially significant. In styles of painting with an advancing observation of nature and a considerable perspective depth the varied directions of the head have also a role in producing an effect of free movement, a fuller possession of the space. But though the choice is less restricted here, the artist gives great weight to the duality of profile and frontal as paired carriers of opposed meanings where such opposition is important, and composes accordingly. In Greek sculpture, in which aesthetic considerations are strong, we often discern this factor of meaning in the choice; in a relief showing an author and his muse, the first is seated in profile and the second stands frontal as if the artist wished to mark different grades of reality in distinguishing a person and a personification. The relative importance of such types of content in the subject matter of art will affect the stylistic norms of bodily direction and the deviations from them.

Returning to our example — Moses at the battle with the Amalekites: we have seen how the artists choose at first a posture of Moses that resembles the symbolized content in form. He stands facing us and his arms are extended like the arms of Christ on the cross. Later he is turned in profile, the reference to the cross is thereby blocked or weakened, and Moses becomes a part of the action like the fighting soldiers who are also shown in profile. The contrast between the symbol-laden frontal posture of Moses and the profile of the other figures is abolished by the uniform profile or near-profile of all the actors. The earlier rendering of Moses as if turned towards us and with arms outstretched appears all the more clearly then as a specially accented form suited to the reading of the episode as a symbol. The historical Moses in this version is not only himself a sign but he makes a sign which is addressed to the Christian viewer with his awareness of the cross; while the later profile pictures an action of which the significance is given in the simple denotation of the words of the Bible and calls for no deeper understanding as a symbol.

In the two Bodleian miniatures (Fig. 20) the contrast of frontal and profile, though less strongly marked than before, is a means of distinguishing a past symbolic event and a present symbolized one, the first a unique historic action and the second a recurrent liturgical performance. I do not mean that all examples of contrasted profile and frontal figures have this function or that a symbolic picture and its represented meaning are commonly distinguished in this way; the duality has been used elsewhere to express different polar ideas. In the Moralized Bible the two postures also correspond to an older and a newer tendency of style, so that one form has a somewhat archaic flavor and the other appears more actual, more modern. In the 12th and 13th centuries we know other examples of the conversion of traditionally frontal figures into profile (or near-profile) ones. The human profile in this art is, in general, the more advanced form and its frequency accords with a trend towards the concrete and active; in older art the frontal form is the more pronounced as a vehicle of the sacred or transcendent.[81] Throughout medieval Christian art it marks what I have called the theme of state and is applied not only in theophanies but to royal persons as well. Even in the later period in images of action a king or spiritually commanding figure is sometimes represented full-face.[82]

In medieval art certain figures were presented either in profile or frontally, and we can gauge through them the different effects of the two views as expressive means. In relief sculptures of the Adoration of the Magi above church doors of the 12th century the Virgin is often enthroned in the center of the field like a cult statue, while the Magi and other figures are set in profile on both sides. A tympanum at Saint-Gilles is an example of this type (Fig. 27). But in some works, as on the delightful portal of Neuilly-en-Donjon in Burgundy (Fig. 27a), the Virgin is off-center and turned to the approaching Magi.[83] She is part of a historic action and not an immobile transcendent figure with a distinct axis of her own. Though the relief at Saint-Gilles is the later work and more developed plastically in the sense of future art, it is the profile solution of the earlier artist that will be followed in paintings of the Virgin and the Magi in the next centuries.

Another and more striking example of the change is the rendering of the story of Daniel in the Lions' Den. In early Christian art and in the first centuries of the Middle Ages, Daniel is a standing figure, frontal and orant, flanked by two lions. When this quasi-heraldic grouping appears in Spanish Mozarabic art, as in the manuscripts of Beatus on the Apocalypse (which include Jerome's commentary on Daniel), we are inclined to see the symmetrical pattern as the product of a folkloric provincial style that converts scenes of action into static ornamental schemes (Fig. 28). But although the drawing and color are primitive, the artist has been faithful to a statuesque classic prototype; the conception of the whole can be traced to the symmetry of a more richly articulated Greco-Roman art. When the same subject was illustrated by a painter of naturalistic tendency in Southern France during the mid-11th century in the Beatus manuscript of Saint-Sever, he gave up the ancient scheme (Fig. 29). He showed Daniel with arms raised in profile as if to receive the food from Habbakuk above him; the gesture of prayer has become ambiguous. Daniel sits at one side in a walled enclosure with seven lions before him in repeated profile. The seated position, new in pictures of the scene, was based on a passage in the Bible (Daniel 14:39) that had been ignored by artists until then, like the reference to seven lions (14:31). The text was read now with more interest in its elements of reality and drama, though the scene retained for the imaginative Christian viewer, even in its episodic form, the old core of symbolism including the eucharistic sense of Habbakuk miraculously transported and bringing bread to Daniel.

These examples and others confirm our belief that the changed illustration of the Moses story is the outcome of more than a change in exegesis. It depends on new norms of representation as well as on a fresh understanding of the text. Though we speak of it as an aesthetic change in style of art, we recognize in it also a change in general outlook and in the attitude to the particular class of objects represented.

A document of the 13th century, in telling of a conservative cleric's resistance to the emerging vogue of the profile, also gives an evidence of the value attached then to the frontal form as both more sacred and more beautiful. A Spanish bishop, Luke of Tuy († 1250), condemned as the work of heretics the new one-eyed image of the Virgin. He thought they wished to express their idea of Christ's humility in choosing to be born of so ugly a mother.[84] I can hardly believe that this explanation, which recalls the classic story of Apelles' unusual profile portrait of the one-eyed king Antigonus, presents the true ground of the bishop's feeling.[85] He would not have objected to the rendering of the Magi in profile in a painting or stone relief. More likely what disturbed him was the new style of art in which the Virgin could appear in the same impersonal unmarked profile of narrative action as the lesser figures. We are not surprised to read elsewhere in the bishop's diatribe that he deplored as heretical the new conception of Christ fixed to the cross with three nails instead of four.[86] He might have seen in the three nails the number of the Trinity, but was repelled by the twisted body, for him an uncustomary and ugly form.

In other arts besides the medieval Christian, profile and frontal are often coupled in the same work as carriers of opposed qualities. One of the pair is the vehicle of the higher value and the other, by contrast, marks the lesser. The opposition is reinforced in turn by differences in size, posture, costume, place, and physiognomy as attributes of the polarized individuals. The duality of the frontal and profile can signify then the distinction between good and evil, the sacred and the less sacred or profane, the heavenly and the earthly, the ruler and the ruled, the noble and the plebeian, the active and the passive, the engaged and the unengaged, the living and the dead, the real person and the image. The matching of these qualities and states with the frontal and profile varies in different cultures, but common is the notion of a polarity expressed through the contrasted positions. Sometimes the body as a whole rather than the face is the carrier of the frontality or profile, sometimes the head more than the body, and there are examples in which the contrast is of profile and three-quarters, of full-face and near-profile, of three-quarters and full-face. The opposition may be of a single figure to a standard presentation of all the others in a group.[87]

In old Egyptian reliefs and paintings where the profile head is the norm for most types of figures, divine and human, the full-face is sometimes given to dancers and musicians and to the dead. Also a minor deity of demonic character, like Bes, is presented full-face. In the system of hieroglyphs the profile head is the sign for 'head', the frontal for 'face' — a distinction interesting for the role of the eyes in the sense of the body and the self.

A Greek vase painting of dancing Maenads before an image of Dionysus shows the maidens in profile, but the ceremonial fetish of the god frontal (Fig. 30). In another vase painting of a mother with her infant and servant, the latter is frontal, and the mother and child are in profile (Figs. 31, 32). More often in Greek art the exceptional frontal figure in a relief or painting — the problem changes in sculpture in the round — is an immobile, passive, or constrained person, one that is withdrawn from action.[88] The full-face is also an attribute of the demonic, particularly of the Gorgons. If Dionysus is presented so in the painting described above, it is not only to distinguish the central object of cult most sharply from the celebrants; it is also because the god is simulated through a fetish — an inert mask and robe set on a stick — in contrast to the living, moving individuals.[89] Where the god himself takes part in an action he is usually drawn in profile. On the pediment in Olympia, Apollo's body in the center of the field is frontal, but his head, in accord with the outstretched right arm that intervenes in the action, is turned in a sharp profile.

In paintings in medieval Arabic manuscripts, which were undoubtedly influenced by Greek tradition, the profile is often reserved for the nobler figure in a pair and the lesser or servile one is in a three-quarters view.[90] One may compare the profile here to the deferential use of the third-person pronoun in European speech. But there are enough examples of the opposite choice to show that the contrast as such is more essential than a fixed value of each term in the pair; what counts is the distinction of rank by a different relation to the viewer.[91]

In Western medieval art the profile is attributed to Judas in the Last Supper, in sharp contrast to the apostles and Christ who are represented in full-face or three quarters. It is also the appearance of demons in opposition to sacred figures in numerous scenes.[92] But in the same styles the pious donor kneels in profile before a majestically enthroned frontal Christ or Virgin.[93] And Satan as a ruler among his subjects may appear in as strict frontality.[94] In the King Louis IX psalter (Paris, Bibl. nat. lat. 10525), where the praying Moses and David are in profile, the evil figures of Ham and Sodomites are also drawn in profile, but in contrast to Noah and Lot who are in three-quarters view.[95] Two senses of the same view may exist then in one style like the variable senses of a word, a grammatical category, or syntactical form in different contexts.[96]

In the choice of profile for demonic and other evil figures one may suppose an aesthetic ground: while the full-face has an ideal closure and roundness — smooth, regular and symmetrical — the profile is indented and asymmetrical and shows a less complete but more sharply characterized face. This was felt by the Spanish bishop who denounced the one-eyed image of the Virgin. The profile was the favored view of the first caricaturists in charging this already broken contour with comic accents and disproportions.[97] But there was perhaps in some uses of the profile in early caricature a nuance of detachment that mitigated the affront of pictorial mockery.

Profile and full-face may be regarded as frameworks within which an artist can reinforce a particular quality of the figure through associated features, while exploiting an effect latent in that view. One could also achieve a powerful expression of polar meanings in opposing to each other two profiles with contrasted features and subtly distinguished glances.

So Giotto in representing the Betrayal of Christ as a dramatic actuality, physical and psychic, replaced the old contrast of profile and frontal, traditional in this subject, by a poignant confrontation of two intensely interacting dissimilar profiles (Figs. 33, 34). A sculptor of the 12th century at Saint-Gilles in Provence had already approached this idea, but merging the tangent profiles of Christ and Judas to form a strange full-face with little sign of feeling, he removed the tension.[98] In Giotto's painting all the figures behind Christ and Judas, except for the profile heads of Peter and Malchus, which reenact with a reduced intensity the opposition of Christ and Judas, are turned towards the center and reinforce the intent glances of the main actors. Only in the narrow space between the profiles of Christ and Judas do we glimpse a frontal face; it is a segment of a face — a nose, eye, and mouth — beside a segment of a profile that overlaps it. Together with the faces of Christ and Judas these interposed heads make a surprising series, a cinematic succession of human features as of a rotating head, passing from the coarse tilted profile of Judas to the noble features of Christ. Giotto's originality of conception will be more evident if we compare his picture with the same scene in the upper church at Assisi, painted a generation earlier (Fig. 35). There Christ's solemn frontal posture detaches him from the profiled Judas and affirms his divine serenity in this turbulent menacing crowd. But the pair lack entirely the inwardness of Giotto's image of the fateful encounter of two men who look into each other's eyes and in that instant reveal their souls. The uncanny power of the glance in a strictly frontal head is transferred to the profile as an objective natural expression, fully motivated in the situation. It is perhaps the first example of a painting in which the reciprocal subjective relations of an I and a You have been made visible through the confrontation of two profiles.

With Giotto in mind one will not take the general shift in art from the stately, often centralized frontal posture to the profile or near-profile of action to be a loss of spiritual depth. Just as a novel written in the third person narrative form can be as revealing of a self as the novel written in the first person which maintains a note of intimate, confiding self-disclosure and brings the narrator close to the reader, so in a painting the profile may carry a subtle expression of a speaking self. The profile portrait, with its more sharply defined and individualized silhouette, has seemed in certain styles and subjects less open to nuances of inner life than the front or three-quarters view.[99] What is specific to the face as a sign of an attentive, responding, or speaking self is not given in every style. As was said before, the full-face is sometimes blind, a schematic mask that is turned towards one but has no penetrating gaze. In many archaic works the frontal stance was only a generalized

posture; the artist had yet to discover the fuller range of physiog-
nomic expression in searching both the human face and the resources
of his art.

The plurality of meaning in each of these two appearances of the
head would seem to exclude a consistent explanation based on
inherent qualities of the profile and the frontal or full-face view.
It is like the difficulty of finding in colors a universal, culturally
unconditioned ground for their symbolic use, though we experience
colors as strongly charged with feeling. Both black and white are
associated with death, and blue is an attribute of the underworld
and of heaven. Travelling through Central Asia, Marco Polo noted
that in a province of India black was the preferred color and white
was reserved for the devil, while among the Tartars the favored
color was white.

The familiar argument from these discrepancies: that color
symbolism is entirely conventional, ignores that a color is not a
simple elementary feature but a complex of qualities of which
certain ones become more or less pronounced in a particular
setting and according to a perceiver's experience and attitude.[100]
A blue which, as the color of the sky in a painting, looks filmy and
soft may appear cold and deep in another painting as the color of
hell. Certain of these qualities will be found in other colors as well.
Besides, we classify as blue many distinct tones, values, and
intensities of blue, with varying modes of appearance; it is a mistake
then to look for a unique root affect residing in the common hue.
The qualities of appearance depend on physical properties of the
individual tones and their obscure physiological effects; but
according to the context, which includes the associated meanings
as well as the relation to neighboring colors, different qualities or
tendencies of a particular blue will be brought into more active play.

So also with black and white, which have striking features in
common. Both are achromatic and extremes of brightness, and in
these respects are interchangeable as symbols, if what has to be
symbolized is an extreme state. Both black and white can convey
the void of death. Either can serve as a negation of the vital, the
growing, the natural. But the sense of each in a specific context of

death is variable; as Plutarch observed in considering different explanations of funerary usage, white clothes are worn by mourners to overcome the blackness of death.[101] By its purity and brightness, white can symbolize the spiritual and innocent; by its lack of color, the inert and cold. [102]

A parallel may be found in the matching of sky and earth or sun and moon with male and female. In Greek and other Western traditions, the sky and sun gods are male and the earth divinity female, as in the gender of words for sky, sun and earth. But in Japan the Shinto ruler of the heavens is a woman. Yet neither choice is entirely arbitrary; we can describe the earth as masculine in its weight, dark soil and hard rock in contrast to the sky, and the sky as feminine in its lightness, softness, and variability. But one can also proceed from other qualities and match the earth's receptiveness and fertility with the woman, and couple the rain-giving, over-arching, sunny sky with man. In both pairings, as in poetic metaphors, real qualities of the symbols and the symbolized are brought out in the contrasted matchings.

Common to these examples of expressive duality is the constraint on matchings inherent in the limited choice. In a representation with a sharply contrasted pair, a quality or meaning of one member as a ground of the image reinforces a pertinent opposed quality in the other. Moses prays while Joshua fights; Moses raising his hands at the battle is the historical antetype of Christ, while the priest at the altar is the living contemporary type. It is especially (though not only) in styles of art with little range of choice — e.g., with a single dominant posture or view of the head, unlike the styles with a richer series of positions — that the extremes of the frontal and the profile can be paired as contrasted signs which accent other oppositions of the two figures. But the use of the polar forms depends also on the weight of the differences they express within a prevailing system of values and on the related frequency of a certain type of theme. We have observed in the later image of Moses praying at the battle how, at a time when the composition of a narrative picture was conceived more and more fully as an objective spectacle in nature detached from the viewer and when the frontal figure became rare or less pronounced in scenes of action, there was an accompanying disregard of the prospective theological meaning. In the 17th century one could easily have rendered the original cross pattern of the praying Moses' raised arms in a foreshortened three-quarters or near-profile view — like the cross itself in certain pictures with side views of the Crucifixion and of Saint Francis receiving the stigmata. But this was not done. For parallel to the shift from frontality to profile the subject itself had lost much of its force as a Christian typological symbol.

# NOTES

[1] I quote this text after Jean Pépin, *Mythe et allégorie* (Paris, 1958), p. 264.

[2] Cf. the example in the recently discovered catacomb in Rome — A. Ferrua, *Le pitture della nuova catacomba di via Latina* (Vatican City, 1960), pl. XV, XCI.

[3] See M. Schapiro, " 'Cain's Jawbone that Did the First Murder' ", *Art Bulletin* 24 (1942), 205-12.

[4] See Henri de Lubac, *L'exégèse médiévale: Les quatre sens de l'Écriture*, 4 vols. (Paris 1959-63).

[5] See Ernest De Wald, *The Utrecht Psalter* (Princeton, n.d.), pl. 40. To illustrate psalm 84 (85):12 — "Truth shall spring out of the earth and righteousness shall look down from heaven", the artist drew the Virgin presenting the Christ child to a personification of Justice — a woman in the sky receiving the child, Truth (*ibid.*, pl. 79, and p. 39 for a corresponding text by Athanasius).

[6] See J. Tikkanen, *Die Psalterillustration im Mittelalter* I (Helsingfors, 1895), p. 63, for examples in the Greek psalters (Chludoff, Barberini, Hamilton) and commentaries.

[7] The artist also elaborates the literal illustration in unexpected ways; e.g., for psalm 25 (26):6 — "I will wash my hands in innocency" — he draws nine figures washing their hands in a big basin filled with water from a sculptured lion's mouth at the end of a Roman aqueduct descending from a high mountain, *ibid.*, pl. 23.

Another remarkable Carolingian manuscript with both the literal and allegorical types of illustration is the Stuttgart Psalter; see E. T. De Wald, *The Stuttgart Psalter* (Princeton, 1930), and F. Mütherich, B. Bischoff, B. Fischer *et al.*, *Der Stuttgarter Bilderpsalter* (Stuttgart, 1968).

[8] As in the Ingeborg psalter in Chantilly; F. Deuchler, *Der Ingeborgpsalter* (Berlin, 1967), pl. VII.

[9] See M. Schapiro, "The Sculptures of Souillac", *Mediaeval Studies in Memory of Arthur Kingsley Porter* (Cambridge, Mass., 1939), 359-87.

[10] See M. Schapiro, "The Angel with the Ram in Abraham's Sacrifice: A Parallel in Western and Islamic Art", *Ars Islamica* 10 (1943), 135-52; and "An Irish-Latin Text on the Angel with the Ram in Abraham's Sacrifice", *Essays in the History of Art Presented to Rudolf Wittkower* (London, 1967), 17-19. In Souillac the faggots carried by Isaac are a rounded bushy bundle of thin branches and could not be taken readily for analogues of the wood of the cross.

[11] I have followed the King James version, but have modernized the words in a few places.

[12]   See T. W. Manson, "The Argument of Prophecy", *Journal of Theological Studies* (1945), 132ff.
[13]   XII, 2, 3. See *The Apostolic Fathers*, ed. by L. Schopp (New York, 1947).
[14]   *Dialogue with Trypho*, ch. 90, 97, 131 — Migne, Pat. gr. VI, cols. 690-91.
[15]   *Adversus Judaeos*, III — *Opera* IV, rec. E. F. Leopold (Leipzig, 1841), p. 317. The same text is repeated in *Adversus Marcionem*, III, c. 18, *ibid.*, III, p. 133.
[16]   *Homilies on Joshua*, cited by Jean Daniélou, *Sacramentum Futuri: Études sur les origines de la typologie biblique* (Paris, 1950), pp. 212-13. See also his *Homilies on Exodus*, XI.
[17]   *Testimonia* II, 21 — *C.S.E.L.*, *Opera Omnia*, rec. G. Hartel, vol. III, 1, p. 89.
[18]   The same idea appears in the writings of Prudentius, *Cathamerinon*, XII; Migne, Pat. lat. LIX, col. 912; Gregory Nazianzen, *Orations*, IV, XIII — Pat. gr. XXXV, cols. 547, 854: Augustine, *De Trinitate*, IV, c. 15, Pat. lat. XLII, col. 901; Maximus of Turin, *Homily L: De cruce Domini*, *ibid.*, LVII, cols. 345-46; Ephraém Syrus, *Commentarii in Genesim et Exodum*, ed. R.-M. Tonneau (Louvain, 1965), pp. 126, 127; and others.
[19]   Philo, who believed that the literal text, like the letter of the Law, is "a symbol of intellectual things", wrote in his *Allegory of the Laws* (III, 186) that the prayer of Moses with lifted arms "signifies that the soul triumphs when it raises itself above the world of sense" (cited by J. Daniélou, *Sacramentum...*, p. 190, n. 1). A later rabbinical author said: "It was not the uplifted arms of Moses that miraculously made Israel prevail. The Scripture teaches that when the Israelites looked upward and subjected their mind and will to their Father in heaven, they prevailed, and when they did not they fell down slain" (*Mekilta Rosh ha-Shanah* 3:8, quoted from George F. Moore, *Judaism in the First Centuries of the Christian Era* II [Cambridge, Mass., 1927], p. 206). Louis Ginzberg has supposed that the rabbinical interpretation was directed against the Christian reading of Exodus 17:12 as a prefiguration of the cross (*The Legends of the Jews* VI, p. 25, n. 145, with references to these and other Jewish texts).
[20]   "Haec autem omnia in figura contingebant illis" is the Vulgate text; the Greek version calls these precedents *typoi*. See also Hebrews 10:1, *umbram enim habens lex futurorum bonorum, non ipsam imaginem rerum*. Paul's idea is already in Wisdom 16:6 where the brazen serpent of Num. 21:8 is called "a sign of salvation and a reminder of the commandment of thy law" *(signum salutis ad commemorationem mandatum legis tuae)*. The brazen serpent is cited in the gospel of John where Jesus says: "And as Moses lifted up the serpent in the desert, so must the Son of Man be lifted up ..." (3:14).
[21]   Another discrepancy is the presence of the hand of God in the sky, to which Moses turns his head. God does not address Moses during the battle, but afterwards in Exodus 17:14.
[22]   The singular form *manum* was not altogether unknown in the Latin world. The editor of Cyprian's *Testimonia* (II, 21 — C.S.E.L., rec. G. Hartel [1868], III, 1, p. 89) cites an exceptional manuscript (of the 8-9th century) with this reading. In the apparatus of variants in the recent Vatican edition of the Latin Bible (ed. H. Quentin) are noted two examples — *sub* Ex. 17:11, 12 — in mediaeval manuscripts.

[23] The Lord says to Moses: "Tu autem eleva virgam tuam, et extende manum tuam super mare, et divide illud."

[24] Cf. Exodus 13:9 — God led the Jews out of Egypt *in manu forti;* Ex. 14:9 — the Israelites departed from Egypt *in manu excelsa;* Ex. 15:6 — Moses' canticle, "Dextera tua, Domine"; and 15:12 — "Extendisti manum tuam et devoravit eos terra". For the raised staff or rod as God's hand see Hugo Gressmann, *Mose und sein Zeit* (Göttingen, 1913), pp. 158-59, and in *Die Schriften des alten Testaments*, II: *Die Anfänge Israels* (Göttingen, 1922), pp. 101-02.

Perhaps significant for a conflation of older texts in Exodus 17 is the fact that the rod is called *Elohim*'s in 17:9, while the hand is *Yahveh*'s in 17:16.

[25] For a figure with both arms raised, cf. the relief of a winged man with an eagle's head from the city gate of Sendjirli — A. Jeremias, *Das alte Testament im Lichte des alten Orients*, 2nd ed. (Leipzig, 1906), Fig. 201, and a relief from Babylon of a god holding in his raised hands an ax and a whip of lightning, *ibid.*, Fig. 44. For the figure (or divine emblem) with raised arms or wings supported by two figures, cf. the relief at Tell Halaf — M. von Oppenheim, *Tell Halaf* (London, n.d.), pl. 8b (our Fig. 7), and the examples reproduced by E. Herzfeld, "Die Kunst des zweiten Jahrtausends in Vorderasien", *Archäologische Mitteilungen aus Iran* 9 (1938), 1ff. and Figs. 124, 132. See also H. P. L'Orange, *Studies in the Iconography of Cosmic Kingship in the Ancient World* (Oslo, 1953), Figs. 65c, 77. In the Greenfield Papyrus (British Museum) of the Egyptian *Book of the Dead* (10th century B.C.) the sky goddess Nut is represented as an arched figure supported by the raised arms of Shu (= air) whose own arms are held up by two smaller bull-headed figures (D. Diringer, *The Illuminated Book* [London, 1958], pl. I, 3b).

[26] An early Christian miracle-working mosaic image of Christ in Ravenna, called "Brachium Forte" was invoked in prayer as the same hand that led the children of Israel out of Egypt — Agnellus, *Liber Pontificalis, Vita Neonis,* Pat. lat., CVI, cols. 519-20. For the raised right hand of power in ancient and Christian art, see L'Orange, *Studies in the Iconography...*, pp. 139ff.

[27] See B. Colgrave, *Eddius Stephanus, Life of Bishop Wilfrid* (Cambridge, 1927), pp. 28-29.

[28] See L. Gougaud, *Christianity in Celtic Lands* (London, 1932), pp. 90, 93, 94, 271, 272, 281. The figure with raised arms appears in pagan Celtic art in a context of combat and hunt on the Gundestrup cauldron and in Scandinavian art on the lost Gallehus horns. For the latter see W. Hartner, *Die Goldhörner von Gallehus* (Wiesbaden 1969), Figs. 1, 1a, 3.

[29] *Monumenta Germaniae historiae*, Epistolae IV, pp. 137ff. Cf. also Alcuin's letter to Charlemagne in 800 on a victory in war: "For Moses, whom you propose to us as an example after having won the battle and put to flight the Amalekites ..." (Pat. lat., C, col. 331, ep. 109); and another letter to archbishop Paulinus (800) on his fight against heretics: "it is for us to help you, with humble prayers, like Moses with hands raised to heaven", *ibid.*, col. 343 (ep. 113).

[30] See Liudprand of Cremona, *Antapodosis*, IV, 24. I quote from *The Works of Liudprand of Cremona* (London, 1930), transl. by F. A. Wright, p. 159.

There is a similar episode in a poem by the deacon Theodosius on the expedition to Crete led by Nicephorus Phocas ca. 960. The king chants psalm 27:1

for God's help; "then you, in battle, acted as Moses once did, who defeated Amalek by raising his hands high" — Pat. gr. CXIII, col. 1035.

[31] See the translation by E. Pognon, *L'an mille* (Paris, 1947), p. 250.

[32] It is reported by Balderic of Dol, *Historia Hierosolymitana*, I. 45, translated by A. Krey, *The First Crusade* (Princeton, 1921), p. 36.

There is perhaps an echo of the crusades in a passage in Alexander Neckam's *De Naturis Rerum*, c. III, following a comment on Ishmael: "Let us pray with Moses, holding up our hands to God, and the true Joshua will fight for us and defeat the Amalekites. Let us then follow the true Joshua as our leader so that the land promised us on high may be allotted to us as the true sons of Israel" (ed. by Thomas Wright [London, 1863], p. 28). For a helpful suggestion in translating this text I wish to thank Professor Harry Caplan of Cornell University.

[33] The inscription refers to "Moses propped up by Aaron and Hur". The miniature is reproduced and described by H. Omont, *Miniatures des plus anciens manuscrits grecs de la Bibliothèque nationale du VIe au XIVe siècle* (Paris, 1929).

[34] See D. Hesseling, *Miniatures de L'Octateuque grec de Smyrne* (Leyden, 1909), pl. 61, no. 185; J. Wilpert, *Die römischen Mosaiken und Malereien* I (Freiburg im Breisgau, 1916), Fig. 468 (Vatican Library ms. gr. 746).

[35] It is *Oration XIII*, on the consecration of bishop Eulalios — Pat. gr. XXXV, col. 854 — "through the symbolical mystic figure of the hands he [Moses] smashed the Amalekite host. The hands of the priest, lifted up on the mountain and posed in prayer, could accomplish what many thousands of men could not do". See also *Oration IV*, against Julian, for the same thought — *ibid.*, col. 547.

There is a remarkable example in a Greek manuscript of the same period in Smyrna, where a picture of Moses at the battle with the Amalekites, with his hands supported by Aaron and Hur, is juxtaposed to a water-scape with an ibis. The accompanying text of the *Physiologus* describes the ibis (Leviticus 11:17) as a bird that does not know how to dive and lives in shallow waters where the impure fishes abide. The Christian moral: "O man! learn to dive deep so that you may reach the depths of the wisdom and knowledge of God. If you do not stretch out your hand and make the sign of the cross, you will never sail over the sea of life. To give light, the sun stretches forth its beams, and the moon its horns; and the bird, to fly, stretches out both wings. Moses, when he stretched out his hands, conquered Amalek; so did Daniel subdue the lions." The writer goes on to cite the examples of Jonah, Thekla, Susanna, Judith, Esther and the Three Boys in the Furnace, all of whom were saved by faith. See J. Strzygowski, *Der Bilderkreis des griechischen Physiologus, des Kosmas Indikopleustes und Oktateuch* (Leipzig, 1899), p. 41. The original text of the *Physiologus* is of the early Christian period and makes no mention of Aaron and Hur whose presence in the illustration, supporting the arms of Moses, is probably a late addition.

[36] On the Farfa Bible, see W. Neuss, *Die Katalanische Bibel illustration* (Bonn, 1922), Figs. 1, 7 (Fig. 1 is mis-labelled as of the Roda Bible). See also Fig. 24 for a copy of the second of these miniatures on the 12th-century sculptured portal of Ripoll in Catalonia.

[37] British Museum, Cotton Ms. Claudius B IV, f. 95v — Arthur Kingsley Porter believed that Moses, Aaron, and Hur were represented still earlier in

the 8th-century Book of Kells on the page (fol. 114) that is usually interpreted as the Arrest of Christ (*The Crosses and Culture of Ireland* [1931], pp. 51-53). His argument that the miniature precedes by two pages the text of the Arrest (Matthew 26:47-50) and therefore cannot be of that subject, overlooks the fact that in the early Middle Ages the chapter divisions were unlike the present ones and that the section with the account of the Arrest began then at 26:30: "Et hymno dicto exierunt in montem Oliveti" (see S. Beissel, *Die Entstehung der Perikopen des römischen Messbuches* [Freiburg im Breisgau, 1907], p. 201), precisely the words inscribed over the Kells miniature. Besides, the subject of Moses has no apparent connection with the text of Matthew 26:30 — Christ in Gethsemane. The type of Arrest in the Book of Kells, with two unarmed men seizing Christ by the arms, agrees with several other early examples: the 6th-century gospels in Cambridge — Corpus Christi College ms 286; an ivory in the Louvre (G. Millet, *Recherches sur l'iconographie de l'évangile* [Paris, 1916], Fig. 333); a Syriac miniature in the British Museum (*ibid.*, Fig. 339), a relief in Raphoe, Ireland (Porter, 1931: Fig. 81), a drawing in the Anglo-Saxon psalter, British Museum Ms. Tiberius C VI, and sculptures on Irish stone crosses at Armagh, Connor and Monasterboice (F. Henry, *La sculpture irlandaise* [Paris, 1933]).

[38] In the Aelfric manuscript Moses sits on a slab of yellow stone, and the kneeling Aaron and Hur support his arms in their veiled hands. Rabanus Maurus, in a commentary on Exodus (Pat. lat., CVIII, cols. 84, 85), likens the stone to the Church; Moses sits on the stone "cum lex requievit in Ecclesia". — A Byzantine writer, George Cedrenus, in describing the battle with the Amalekites in his compendium of history, has Aaron and Hur support Moses by placing stones under his hands (Pat. gr. CXXI, col. 170) — perhaps a copyist's defective reading of Cedrenus' text.

[39] "Quia manus solii Domini ... erit contra Amalek" (cf. also Exodus 17:14). The Latin is an arbitrary version of the Hebrew text which is itself obscure and perhaps referred simply to the hand holding the rod as the Lord's standard or sign.

[40] On this miniature in Munich Staatsbibliothek lat. 4456, see George Swarzenski, *Die Regensburger Buchmalerei* (Leipzig, 1901), pp. 64-65, 73-74; and P. E. Schramm and F. Mütherich, *Denkmale der deutschen Könige und Kaiser* (Munich, 1962), p. 157, no. 111.

[41] Bamberg, Staatsbibliothek lit. 53, *ibid.*, p. 159, no. 117. See also the *Pericope Book of Henry III* (1039-43) from Echternach for a similar picture of the emperor and his mother Gisela — Bremen Staatsbibliothek B 21 (*ibid.*, p. 173, no. 153, and A. Goldschmidt, *German Book Illumination* II [New York, n.d.], pl. 53).

[42] See P. E. Schramm, "Das Herrscherbild in der Kunst des frühen Mittelalters", *Vorträge der Bibliothek Warburg* I *(1922-23)*, (1924), p. 210 and notes 216, 221. A similar ceremony is described by Geoffrey of Monmouth in his imaginary account of the coronation of King Arthur — *Historia Regum Britanniae*, IX (ed. by Griscom and Jones, p. 455).

[43] See O. Treitinger, *Die Oströmische Kaiser-und Reichsidee vom Oströmische Staats- und Reichsgedanken*, 2nd ed. (Darmstadt, 1956), pp. 130ff., 133; and A. Grabar, *L'empereur dans l'art byzantin* (Paris, 1936), pp. 95-97. J. Tikkanen

(*Psalterillustration* I [1895], p. 45) notes that in the Byzantine psalter (British Museum Add. Ms. 19352), Moses' rod at the miracles of the Red Sea and the rock of Horeb is a cross staff and that Byzantine liturgy refers to the rod as a type of the cross. In the Syriac *Book of the Bee*, the rod is said to be a branch of the tree of knowledge, transmitted to Moses by way of Abraham, Joseph of Nazareth, and Judas Iscariot; it served as the transverse beam of the cross (M. Grünbaum, *Neue Beiträge zur semitischen Sagenkunde* [Leiden, 1893], pp. 162-63).

[44] Grabar, 1936: pl. XXIII. For the role of prayer and religious rites in Byzantine warfare, see J. R. Vieillefond, "Les pratiques religieuses dans l'armée byzantine d'après les traités militaires", *Revue des Études Anciennes* 37 (1935), 322-30. He cites an anonymous 10th-century Byzantine text on military tactics in which the general charges certain officers to preach to the army, to "proclaim that the victories fulfill the prophecies of the saints and to predict the defeat of the enemy according to the sacred books" (p. 326).

[45] For the texts and images, see L'Orange, 1953: Figs. 76, 78-80. A parallel to this modelling of the pictures of Old Testament ceremonial on actual state ceremonies of the day, and the variation of those pictures with changes in ideological and political relations of church and state, appear in the conception of images of the Anointing of David by Samuel in medieval art. In Early Christian and Byzantine art David always stands in pictures of this subject. In the West, ever since the anointing and papal crowning of the Carolingian rulers, David often kneels (cf. the miniature in the Stuttgart psalter); and where he is shown seated on his throne in this scene we suspect sometimes, besides the assimilation to contemporary ceremony, an assertion of the monarch, and in the standing posture a conservative copying of an old Byzantine model. See M. Schapiro, "An Illuminated English Psalter of the 13th Century", *Journal of the Warburg and Courtauld Institutes* 23 (1960), 181ff.

[46] *Mon. Germ. Hist.*, Ep., III, 1, p. 505, no. 11; see also p. 552, no. 39; p. 554, no. 42; and p. 649, no. 98.

[47] *Mon. Germ. Hist.*, pp. 479-80, no. 3. See also ep. no. 33. In a letter to Pippin, addressing him as a "New Moses", Pope Paul I quotes psalm 88 (89):22: *ecce manus eius auxiliabitur tui, et brachium ipsius confortabit te*, changing the pronouns to shift the reference from David to Pippin — *ibid.*, p. 555.

[48] Cf. the formula of Charlemagne: *Ego Karolus rex et rector regni Francorum et devotus sancti Dei ecclesiae defensor humilisque adiutor*, quoted by P. E. Schramm, *Kaiser, Könige und Päpste* I (Stuttgart, 1968), pp. 184-85. The idea that the royal power is obligated to aid the church was expressed earlier in a letter of Bede to bishop Ecgbert, *Opera Historica Bedae* I, ed. by C. Plummer, p. 412.

[49] See p. 20 above and n. 25.

[50] See *Antique Works of Art from Benin*, collected by General Pitt-Rivers (London, 1900), pl. 2, fig. 7; pl. 12, fig. 76, etc.

[51] As on the reliefs on the tympana of S. Isidoro in León (A. K. Porter, *Romanesque Sculpture of the Pilgrimage Roads* [Boston, 1923], ill. 702) and St. Sernin in Toulouse (*ibid.*, ill. 308-10). There is a pagan parallel in an ivory carving of the 5th century A.D. with a scene of apotheosis of a ruler who is lifted up by two winged figures (W. F. Volbach, *Elfenbeinarbeiten der Spätantike*

*und des frühen Mittelalters*, 2nd ed. [Mainz, 1952], nr. 56, pl. 14). But a Biblical source may be found in Psalm 90 (91):12 — "angels shall bear thee up in their hands". In the Utrecht Psalter, f. 10v, ps. 18 (19), (De Wald, n.d.: pl. XVI), Christ is drawn with arms supported by two angels at the door of the temple, to illustrate verse 6, "as a bridegroom coming out of his bride chamber". In the Winchester Psalter, British Museum Cotton Ms. Nero C IV, in the scene of the Doubting Thomas (f. 26), two apostles hold up Christ's extended arms.

52   See Porter, 1923: ill. 152-55. For a related conception in the old Orient, cf. the throne in the reliefs at Persepolis (L'Orange, 1953: Figs. 56, 58-60). There may be an echo of this image merged with that of the enthroned Byzantine ruler in a picture and text of the Lapidary of Alfonso X in the Escorial Library. The miniature shows a man, with arms raised, sitting on a four legged bench held up by four winged men. According to the text the picture represents the power that heaven (Jupiter) will give to one who finds at the astrologically right time the precious stone called *yarganza amariella*. There existed perhaps a gem engraved with such an image of the enthroned ruler. See the facsimile edition: *Lapidario del rey Alfonso X* (Madrid, 1883), fol. 102.

53   It is the painting now in the Pitti Gallery in Florence. The picture was perhaps inspired in part by passages in the psalms, e.g., 17(18):10 — "and he rode upon a cherub, and did fly"; 98 (99):1 — "he sitteth between the cherubims", which is followed in 98:6 by reference to Moses and Aaron — "They called upon the Lord and he answered them".

54   British Museum Add. Ms. 11639, f. 525v. It is a collection of Bible readings, prayers, and other texts. See G. Margoliouth, *Hebrew and Samaritan Manuscripts in the British Museum*, Part III (1915), pp. 402ff. B. Narkiss (*Hebrew Illuminated Manuscripts* [New York, 1969], p. 86) dates it "c. 1280" and places it in "Troyes (?)".

55   The text is of the 14th century poet Shahin — see the *Encyclopedia Judaica* 9 (Berlin 1939), col. 565, and the frontispiece for a color reproduction of this page. The way of raising the arms, close to the sides of the body, also weakens the analogy to the cross; but a similar gesture appears in the second drawing of the scene in the Farfa Bible and is often ascribed to Christ in the Last Judgment where the wounds on the hands are more pointedly exposed in this position. I owe my knowledge of the Shahin miniature to the kindness of Professor Rachel Wischnitzer.

56   See Louis Ginzberg, *The Legends of the Jews* in note 19; also Marcel Simon *Verus Israel: Études sur les relations entre Chrétiens et Juifs dans l'Empire Romain (135-425)* (Paris, 1948).

57   Simon, 1948: 191.

58   See Carl Kraeling, *The Synagogue (The Excavations at Dura-Europos*, VIII, 1; *Final Report)* (New Haven, 1956), Fig. 58, p. 222. The crossing of the hands is clearly marked in the 4th-century painting in the recently discovered catacomb of the Via Latina in Rome; A. Ferrua, *Le pitture della nuova catacomba di via Latina* (Vatican City, 1960), pl. XXV.

59   See *Il Rotulo di Giosué, Codice Vaticano Palatino Greco 431* (Milan, 1905), pl. 13, 14, 19; K. Weitzmann, *The Joshua Roll* (Princeton, 1948), pl. IV, fig. 34; pl. XIII, fig. 46; A. Goldschmidt and K. Weitzmann, *Die byzantinischen Elfenbeinskulpturen des X-XIII Jahrhunderts* (Berlin, 1930), pl. 1, 2; S. Cirac Esto-

pañan, *Skyllitzes Matritensis,* I; *Reproducciones y Miniaturas* (Barcelona-Madrid, 1965), f. 98v, no. 228 — for a later hanging on a forked stake.

[60] Th. Mommsen, *Römisches Strafrecht* (Leipzig, 1899), p. 921.

[61] "... deposuerunt cadaver eius de cruce".

[62] Cf. the Moralized Bible, Bodleian ms. 270b, f. 99v, where the king of Ai hangs by the neck from a gallows beam set in a forked stake. It is coupled with a scene of Christ on the cross, but the text speaks of the victory of the spiritual over the wicked through Christ's crucifixion; Joshua stands with raised shield (as in 8:18, 19 — a mistranslation of the Hebrew for spear) beside the hanging king.

[63] As on the Klosterneuburg altar; F. Röhrig, *Der Verduner Altar* (Vienna, 1955), pl. 31. These two plaques do not belong to the original work of 1181 by Nicholas of Verdun but were added in the early 14th century. In the Morgan Library Picture Bible of the 13th century (see the new edition, *Old Testament Miniatures*, with text by S. Cockerell and preface by John Plummer, [New York, 1969], pp. 64, 65), the gallows of the king of Ai has a cross-arm, but the whole is tilted diagonally on a pivoted contrivance, perhaps to distinguish it from the cross. S. Cockerell, in editing this manuscript, misinterpreted the gallows as a military engine. The same instrument, tilted diagonally, is represented in the Bodleian Moralized Bible on f. 202, 204, in the scene of the hanging of Haman. The vulgate text of Esther 5:14, illustrated there, also refers to the gallows as *crux (iussit excelsam parari crucem* [5:14]; *ipsum iussi affigi cruci* [8:7]). Haman on the gallows is likened to those who suffer torture in hell for having tortured others.

On the other side, the Jewish legend of Haman assimilated his cross to that of Christ (see L. Ginzberg, *The Legends of the Jews* VI, p. 479, n. 184) and in response the Theodosian codex (408 A.D.) prohibited the Jews from celebrating the Purim feast in which the crucifixion and burning of Haman in effigy were understood to be a mocking of Christ. Under Basil I (ca. 871-875) the formula of abjuration of Judaism by converts in Byzantium still refers to the mocking of Haman on a gibbet surmounted by a cross in the Purim celebration (see L. Bréhier, *La civilisation byzantine* [Paris, 1950], p. 303).

Edgar Wind ("The Crucifixion of Haman", *Journal of the Warburg and Courtauld Institutes* 1 (1937-38), 245-48) has argued ingeniously that Michelangelo, in representing Haman as crucified (on the Sistine ceiling), saw him as a tragic type and forerunner of Christ, in the sense of Frazer's thesis concerning the scapegoat or sacrificed redeemer. However, in Michelangelo's fresco Haman is nailed to a Y-shaped stake, with one leg free and bent and the whole body foreshortened, in a manner that suggests the thief who was crucified beside Christ in Renaissance compositions; and since, moreover, Haman on the ceiling is the counterpart at the left to the brazen serpent that symbolizes Christ at the right, one can interpret Michelangelo's thought in another sense: that the crucified Haman who wished to destroy the Jews is no innocent victim or redeemer but the evil opposite of the brazen serpent that heals and saves.

[64] See H. Omont, *Psautier de Saint Louis: Reproduction des 92 miniatures du ms. latin 10525* (Paris, n.d.), pl. XXIX, LX, LXXIX.

[65] On Joseph as a type of Christ, see M. Schapiro, "The Joseph Scenes on the

Maximianus Throne", *Gazette des Beaux Arts*, 6th series, 40 (1952), 27-38.
[66] See A. de Laborde, *La Bible Moralisée Illustrée* (Paris 1911-27), 5 vols.
[67] Honorius Augustodunensis, *Gemma Animae* I, cap. xliv, xlv, Pat. lat., CLXXII, cols. 557-58. For a similar comparison of Moses' raised hands with those of the priests and bishops in prayer, which assure victory to the faithful, see the *Commentary on Exodus* by Bruno of Asti (early 12th century), Pat. lat., CLXIV, cols. 271-72. Interesting for the shift to the ecclesiastical interpretation is that Bruno takes account here of Exodus 17:9 and says that Moses stands on the hill top holding the rod in his hand as the bishops and those on the higher thrones of the Church carry a staff in their hands for the correction and guidance of the faithful. The likeness of Moses to the priest at the mass is affirmed by Peter Comestor in his re-telling of the story in the *Historia Scholastica*, Exodus Ch. XXXV, Pat. lat., CXCVIII, col. 1161: "in huius rei figura sacerdos manus elevat in missa, etiam in figura Christi orantis in cruce". Pertinent to the liturgical symbolism is also the explanation in the *Glossa Ordinaria*, a compilation of the 12th century (Pat. lat., CXIV, cols. 242-43) — Moses' hands are raised not outstretched. To raise the hands is an act of raising oneself to God" ... elevat manus, non extendit ... Elevare manus hoc est actus levare ad Deum ... Elevat ergo manus qui thesaurizat in coelo" — an interpretation that recalls the rabbinical comments cited above in note 19. But the Gloss also compares the raised hands with the passion of Christ and the defeat of the devil. For the acquaintance of Christian scholars of the 12th century with Jewish exegesis see Beryl Smalley, *The Study of the Bible in the Middle Ages* (University of Notre Dame Press, 1964), pp. 149ff. and 161ff. on Andrew of St. Victor. For the pictorial parallel there is a miniature in the Hortus Deliciarum of Herrade of Landsberg (1167-95), showing Moses at the battle, standing behind an altar, with arms held up by Aaron and Hur — see *Herrade de Landsberg, Hortus Deliciarum*, ed. by A. Straub and G. Keller (Strasbourg, 1901), pl. XIVbis (Supplément).

Another liturgical interpretation interesting for the new symbolism of the scene is that of the exegetist Hugo of St. Cher (+ 1263): "it is because the weary Moses prays sitting that the elders in the church of Paris sit during the Secret of the Mass and in this posture also symbolize the apostles sitting while Christ prays on the Cross; in many churches the old and young stand alike and express thereby Joshua and his army fighting against Amalek" (Hugonis de Sancto Charo, *Opera Omnia* [Venice, 1703], I, p. 86).
[68] For this Bible see Max Friedlaender, *Die Lübecker Bibel* (Munich, 1923). Cf. also the Catalonian miniature of the 14th century in Paris (H. Omont, *Psautier illustré: Reproduction des 107 miniatures du manuscrit latin 8846 de la Bibliothèque Nationale* [Paris, n.d.], pl. 76, psalm 114); the 15th-century Castilian Bible of the Duke of Alba (Roxburghe Club facsimile [Madrid, 1918-21], I, opp. p. 187).

An early example is a drawing in an immense picture Bible from Pamplona (Harburg ms. I,2, lat. 4°, 15, f. 59v), made for Sancho the Strong, king of Navarre (1194-1234). Aaron in near-profile stands at the left with a tau staff, like an abbot's, and Moses kneels at the right with hands raised in profile. An inscription reads: "Moyses orat". The battle takes place below. See François Bucher, *The Pamplona Bibles* II (New Haven, 1970), pl. 122.

[69] Cf. the Bible of Sixtus IV (Venice, apud Juntas, 1616), p. 60; and a Bible of 1603 (Venice, Damianus Zenarius), p. 50.

[70] In a painting by Poussin in the Hermitage, Leningrad, Moses is shown in a near-frontal view with arms extended beside the kneeling Aaron and Hur; but it was not Poussin's intention to present the episode as a symbolic one through Moses' posture, for he has reduced Moses to a barely visible figure far off in the distance while the battle itself occupies the whole foreground and middle depth. The painting is rightly labelled: "The Victory of Joshua over the Amalekites". See A. Blunt, *Nicholas Poussin* II (New York, 1967), pl. 5.

[71] It is now in the church of St. Remi in Reims.

[72] For the interest of Christian scholars in the Hebrew text of the Bible during the later Middle Ages, see B. Smalley, 1964: 338ff. See also note 22 above on the rare occurrence of the singular *manum* in this context at an earlier date.

[73] See p. 61 of the facsimile (n. 63 above); the inscription reads: "Qualiter Amalech bellum infert filiis israel et Iosue iubente Moyse instructa acie occurrit hostibus". Nevertheless in the picture of Abraham's Sacrifice (p. 35), Isaac is shown with two crossed bundles of faggots, the angel crosses his arms in staying Abraham's sword and pointing to the ram, and the latter's horns are caught between two branches of a tree. Yet these details are so little stressed that one may explain them as devices of composition, utilizing older models, without a primary symbolical content.

[74] The same woodcut was used in the Lyons Bible of 1538, printed by Trechsel, and in other Bibles. The crossed hands still appear in the St. Louis Psalter, Bibl. nat. lat. 10525 (Omont, n.d.: pl. XXVII). In Queen Mary's Psalter in the British Museum, an English book of the early 14th century, the blessing itself is not shown but only the after-effect on the feelings of Joseph and his sons. The French text says that Joseph was incensed because the blessing had been given to Ephraim whom he loved less. See Sir George Warner, *Queen Mary's Psalter* (London, 1912), pl. 37 and p. 66. (Perhaps after the expulsion of the Jews from England in 1290 the symbolism of the episode had lost its polemical interest.) Already in the 12th century Peter Comestor in re-telling the story makes no reference to the cross or the Messiah or Christ (*Historia Scholastica*, ch. 101). On the history of the illustration of this subject see W. Stechow, "Jacob Blessing the Sons of Joseph", *Gazette des Beaux-Arts* 23 (1943), 193-208.

[75] *De Legibus* 17 (I, 48-49). I cite this text after the valuable little work of Johan Chydenius, *The Theory of Medieval Symbolism* (= *Societas Scientiarum Fennicarum, Commentationes Humanarum Litterarum* XXVII:2) (Helsingfors, 1960), pp. 20-2.

[76] *The Uniqueness of the Individual* (New York, 1958) p. 74.

[77] As on the ivory cover of the Drogo Sacramentary (ca. 830), where all the figures in the nine scenes of ritual are in profile (A. Goldschmidt, *Die Elfenbein-skulpturen* I [Berlin, 1914], pl. XXX, no. 80b). Also in the miniature paintings in the same manuscript (W. Koehler, *Die Karolingischen Miniaturen* III [Berlin, 1960], pl. 83e, 84b). Carolingian art is in many respects a classic revival like the Latin poetry of the same time and conceives the ritual as an action of the priest or bishop much as the Roman artist, before the age of Constantine, represented ceremonies on the arches of triumph. For the later examples see the psalter, Paris, Bibliothèque de l'Arsenal ms. 1186 (H. Martin, *Psautier de Saint Louis et*

*Blanche de Castille* [Paris, n.d.], pl. 43, for the near-profiles of the priests at the altar, and pl. 20, for the strict profiles of the Jews worshipping the golden calf, while a Christ in three-quarters view gives the tablet to a near-frontal Moses).

[78] A comparable conception of the ritual as exhibiting the hierarchical relations is the pair of ivory plaques of the 9th century in Frankfurt and Cambridge, England, with a beautiful gradation from frontal to profile, large to small, in two liturgical scenes (Goldschmidt, 1914: pl. LIII).

[79] Such an image of Christ in the church of Hagia Sophia is described by Jacopo Voragine in the chapter of the *Golden Legend* on the Feast of the Finding of the Cross (May 3). This appearance of the frontal head was noted also by Nikolaos Mesarites in his *ekphrasis* on the mosaics of the church of the Holy Apostles in Constantinople (ca. 1200); he says of the Pantokrator image on the dome: "His look is gentle and wholly mild, turning neither to the left nor the right, but wholly directed toward all at once and at the same time toward each individually" (transl. by G. Downey, *Transactions of the American Philosophical Society*, N.S. 47 [1957], 870). In the preface of his *De Visione Dei*, Nicholas of Cusa cites as examples of an all-seeing image a bowman aiming an arrow in the marketplace of Nuremberg, Roger van der Weyden's work in the Town Hall in Brussels, a St. Veronica in Brixen, and for his teaching proposes an icon of God as all-seeing, the eyes seeming to move and follow the observer. There is also a Hebrew Midrashic text in which God is likened to a statue that looks at everyone (N. Glatzer, *Hammer on the Rock* [New York], p. 41). Pliny already notes this effect in his *Natural History* 35:37, in writing of the artist Famulus; he painted a Minerva "who faced the spectator at whatever angle she was looked at". The same effect was attributed in the 2nd century A.D. to an idol in Lucian's work *On the Syrian Goddess*, 32 — "And there is still another astonishing thing about this idol: if one stands directly in front of it, she looks at you and follows you when you change your position. And if from another point a new spectator fixes his eyes on her, the goddess will also look at him." The phenomenon was described by Ptolemy in his *Optics*, a work that was available to the Latin West since the 12th century in a translation by the Sicilian admiral Eugenius: "It is thought that the image of a face painted on a tablet looks at the viewer though the image does not move, since a true glance is discerned only through the stability of the form of the same visual ray that falls on the depicted face ... When therefore the viewer moves, the ray of vision moves and the viewer thinks the image is following him with its glance, while he is viewing it" (from the Latin translation by Ammiraglio Eugenio, ed. by G. Govi [Turin, 1885], p. 55).

[80] *Correspondances.* Cf. also the lines of Gérard de Nerval in *Vers Dorés:*

> Crains, dans le mur aveugle un regard qui t'épie
>
> . . . . . . . . . . . . . . .
>
> Et comme un oeil naissant couvert par ses paupières,
> Un pur esprit s'accroît sous l'écorce des pierres!

The uncanny glance of the frontal eyes in a portrait head is a theme in Gogol's *The Portrait*, and Mathurin's *Melmoth the Wanderer*.

[81] Around 1200 the standard profile view of animals and especially of horses and lions is sometimes replaced by a foreshortened front view of the entire

figure — an example of the growing interest in spatial depth and perspective. Earlier there existed the type of profile animal body with frontal head, and in medieval heraldry one came to distinguish the lion from the leopard by the latter's frontal head, both animals having profile bodies (see J. Klanfer, "Theorie des heraldischen Zeichen", p. 73, an unpublished doctoral thesis [Vienna University], for a copy of which I am indebted to the kindness of Dr. F. Novotny).

[82]  In a marginal drolerie in ms. 78 D 40, Royal Library, The Hague, a fox in Franciscan dress and a wolf in Dominican kneel in profile before a crowned frontal lion; Lillian M. C. Randall, *Images in the Margins of Gothic Manuscripts* (Berkeley, 1966), Fig. 497.

[83]  For the different conceptions of this theme, see R. Hamann, "Die Salzwedeler Madonna", *Marburger Jahrbuch für Kunstwissenschaft* 3 (1927), 77-144, pl. XXVIII-LXIII, and especially pl. XLIII, XLIV.

[84]  "Adversus Albigensium Errores", *Maxima Bibliotheca Veterum Patrum* XXV (Lyons, 1677), 222.

[85]  Quintilian, *De Institutione Oratoria*, II, xiii, 12.

[86]  *op. cit.*, p. 223ff. — "ad derisum et opprobrium Christi".

[87]  On the role of the glance, both profile and frontal, in the group portraits of the 16th and 17th century where it is a major factor in the structure and expression of the painting, see the still too little known work of Alois Riegl, *Das holländische Gruppenporträt*, 2nd ed. (Vienna, 1931). I may note here that in the painting of the later 19th and early 20th century, the starkly frontal face and the pairing of frontal and profile returned as elements of the strong expressionist trend, both in portraits and narrative themes. The frontal position in subjects of sorrow, death, jealousy, anxiety, panic, and despair by Munch and Ensor is a means in portraying the person in distress, self-isolating and turned away from others — he cannot 'face' the world; it is also a means of engaging the viewer's attention to the subject's face as that of another and kindred self preoccupied with its own overpowering feelings and speaking out to the viewer. A different use of the contrast of frontal and profile, in a subtle novellistic spirit, is the painting by Vuillard: "The Artist's Mother and Sister" (ca. 1900, Museum of Modern Art, New York) where, in a marked perspective, the mother in black sits in front view before a massive reddish bureau in a plane parallel to the picture surface; the shy daughter, in a shrinking profile, stands at the side close to the mottled papered wall with which she seems to merge through her patterned dress. A few years before, the Impressionist Renoir portrayed a daughter frontally and the mother at the side, without tension.

[88]  On profile and full-face in Greek art, see M. Hoernes, *Urgeschichte der bildenden Kunst in Europa*, 3rd ed. (Vienna, 1925), pp. 592ff., and H. Kenner, *Weinen und Lachen in der griechischen Kunst* (= *Österreichische Akademie der Wissenschaft, Philos.-hist. Kl., Sitzungsberichte* 234, Bd.2 (Vienna, 1960), pp. 40ff.

[89]  For the contrast of the living figure and the image within a representation, there is an interesting example in a Greek vase painting with an actor in profile holding in his hands a frontal mask (K. Schefold, *Classical Greece* [London, 1967], color plate). Cf. also an early Christian sarcophagus fragment in Florence with a relief of Nebuchadnezzar and the three Hebrew boys all in profile before the frontal sculptured head of an idol (*Zeitschrift für Kirchengeschichte* 54

(1935), 18ff. and pl. I). In Titian's portrait of the so-called 'Schiavone', there is a reverse choice: the living woman is frontal and the nearby relief is of a profile bust of a woman, perhaps a relative of the main subject. The choice here may depend on a convention for representing together a major and a minor figure in a double portrait, as in Domenico Ghirlandaio's of Francesco Sassetti and his little son in the Metropolitan Museum in New York.

[90]    See E. Kühnel, *Miniaturmalerei im Islamischen Orient* (Berlin, 1923), pl. 3, 4, 5.

[91]    Kühnel, 1923: Pl. 1, 7, and R. Ettinghausen, *Arab Painting* (1962), pp. 71, 85. There are examples with all figures in profile; Kühnel, pl. 10, 11. But as in Western medieval art the three-quarters head is the common form and the profile and front views are the marked variants. The profile sometimes appears in a corner or near the frame and helps to accent a direction of action.

[92]    Cf. "The Sculptures of Souillac", cited above, note 9. For details see A. K. Porter, *Romanesque Sculpture* (1923), ill. 347, 348. In the Stuttgart Psalter, f. 126 (see the DeWald facsimile), Judas is frontal and is struck by the profiled Satan; in the Moralized Bible, Bodleian ms. 270b, f. 7v, Satan, pictured as an idol in a painting with shutters like an altarpiece, is in profile, and the figures worshipping him are in strict profile.

[93]    Cf. the pictures in the manuscript of the *Cantigas de S. Maria* in the Escorial; J. Guerrero Lovillo, *Miniatura Gotica Castellana, siglos XIII y XIV* (Madrid, 1956), pl. 4, 5, 6, 8, 9.

[94]    As in the Beatus Apocalypse of Saint-Sever, Paris Bibl. nat. ms. lat. 8878, f. 145v — W. Neuss, *Die Apokalypse des hl. Johannes in der altspanischen und altchristlichen Bibel-Illustration* (Münster i.W., 1931), fig. 137.

[95]    Omont, n.d. pl. IV, VIII, XI, LX, LXXXV. A particularly clear example of the use of frontal, three-quarters and profile positions in a narrative picture as distinctions of spiritual and social rank is the fresco of St. Clement in the church of his name in Rome. (See L. Coletti, *Die frühe Italienische Malerei* [Vienna, 1949], pl. 9). The bishop-saint with raised arms at the altar is strictly frontal; the congregation around him are in three-quarters or near-frontal view; the slave who leads away the blinded pagan antagonist Sisinnius is in profile; below, the blind pagan, in near frontal posture, orders in abusive vernacular the arrest of Clement; instead, the slaves in profile bind and carry off a heavy column.

[96]    This duality of the position or view should not be confused with the idea of Freud — a mistaken one, I believe (see E. Benveniste, "Remarques sur la fonction du langage dans la découverte freudienne", *Psychanalyse* 1 [1956], 3-16, now reprinted in *Problèmes de la linguistique générale* [Paris, 1968], 75-87), that in primitive language the same word had contradictory meanings *(Gegensinn der Urworte)*, like certain symbols in dreams. In pictures the profile and frontal are positions with respect to a viewer, that distinguish and accent by contrast the already fixed meanings and qualities of represented objects. Frontal and profile here are more like stress in speech or like the expressive use of the initial position for a word in a sentence, in departure from ordinary syntax.

[97]    For an early example cf. the profile heads of Caiaphas and other Jews, in contrast to the three-quarters head of Christ, in the *Hours of Salisbury*, ca. 1280; E. G. Millar, *English Illuminated Manuscripts from the Xth to the XIIIth*

*century* (Brussels, 1926), pl. 97. Cf. also in a mid-14th-century manuscript of canon law, British Museum Royal 6 E VII, f. 341, the picture of Christians in three-quarters view arguing with heretics and Jews who have strictly profile heads with caricatured features — B. Blumenkranz, *Le juif médiéval au miroir de l'art chrétien* (Paris, 1966), Fig. 26, p. 33. In a Bible of the late 12th century — Paris, Bibl. nat. lat. 16746, f. 80v (possibly from Troyes) — Paul addressing the Jews sits in profile with legs crossed, but his head is a beautiful full face, while the Jews are sharply characterized in their profile heads.

[98]   A. K. Porter, 1923: ill. 1320.

[99]   Thus the expressiveness of Goya's portrait (in the Minneapolis Museum) of himself undergoing a heart-attack is inconceivable in a profile or near-profile view.

[100]   On this aspect of color see the important work of G. J. von Allesch, *Die aesthetische Erscheinungsweise der Farben* (Berlin, 1925).

[101]   *Roman Questions* XXVI, transl. by H. J. Rose (1924), p. 131.

[102]   A parallel to this equipollence of black and white as symbolic colors is the use of both square and circle as models of divine being in religious imagination. Irenaeus says of certain gnostics: "as by some similitude of a sphere or a square, they affirm the Father to comprehend within himself all ways, in the likeness of a sphere or in a quadrangular form" (Irenaeus, *Five Books against Heresies*, transl. by J. Keble [1972], p. 125).

The varying symbolic sense of an object, rooted in its multiple qualities, was recognized by medieval writers who noted, e.g., that the lion could stand for both Satan and Christ. Cf. Peter of Poitiers: "As many significations of spiritual and invisible things can be discovered in corporeal and visible ones as these have properties, whether of inner nature or external form" (in rebus visibilibus... tot possunt reperiri spiritualium rerum et invisibilium significationes quot in ipsis visibilibus et corporalibus rebus inveniuntur proprietates, sive intus in natura, sive in forma foris) — see *Peter Pictavensis Allegoriae super Tabernaculum Moysi*, ed. by Ph. S. Moore and J. A. Corbett (Notre Dame, Indiana, 1938), cap. I, p. 3. Similarly, his contemporary, Alexander Neckam, observed that the symbolism of the serpent (= Satan, Christ, prudence, the year, etc.) varied "secundum diversarum naturarum schemata" of the creature (*De naturis rerum*, cap. CIX — de vulgari serpente — ed. Thomas Wright [London, 1863], p. 190).

Fig. 1. Utrecht Psalter, psalm 43 (44), Utrecht University Library ms. 484, fol. 25.

Fig. 2. Oxford, Bodleian Library, ms. 270b, fol. 15v, Moralized Bible.

Fig. 3. Oxford, Bodleian Library, ms. 270b, fol. 16, Moralized Bible.

Fig. 4. Rome, Sta. Maria Maggiore, nave mosaic.

Fig. 5. Rome, Catacomb of Priscilla, Orant.

Fig. 6. Rome, Catacomb of the Jordani, Daniel.

Fig. 7. Tell Halaf, Hittite relief.

Fig. 8. Paris, Bibliothèque Nationale, ms. grec. 510, fol. 424v, Homilies of Gregory Nazianzen.

Fig. 9. Vatican Library, ms. lat. 5729, Farfa Bible, fol. 1.

Fig. 10. Munich, Staatsbibliothek lat. ms. 4456, fol. 11, Sacramentary of
Henry II.

Fig. 11. Bamberg, Staatliche Bibliothek, lit. 53, fol. 2v, Pontifical of Henry II.

Fig. 12. Paris, Bibliothèque Nationale, ms. lat. 11961, fol. 7, Gospels.

זה משה ואהרן וחור יאשר נוטע ידיו"

Fig. 13. London, British Museum Add. ms. 11639, f. 525v.

Fig. 14. Berlin, Staatsbibliothek, Judeo-Persian ms. by Shahin.

Fig. 15. Vienna, Nationalbibliothek, cod. theol. XXXI, fol. 23, Genesis.

Fig. 16. Dura-Europos, Synagogue, fresco.

Fig. 17. Paris, Bibliothèque Nationale, ms. lat. 10525, Moses at battle.

Fig. 18. Paris, Bibliothèque Nationale, ms. lat. 10525, Joseph revealing himself to his brothers.

Fig. 19. Paris, Bibliothèque Nationale, ms. lat. 10525, Joseph lowered into well.

Fig. 20. Oxford, Bodleian Library 270b, fol. 51v, Moralized Bible, Moses, Aaron, Hur.

Fig. 21. Lübeck Bible, wood cut, 1494, Moses at battle.

Fig. 22. Reims, St. Remi, floor tile from St. Nicaise, Moses, Aaron, and Hur.

Fig. 23. Latin Bible of 1560, woodcut, after Holbein, Jacob blessing the sons of Joseph.

Fig. 24. Kassel, Art Gallery, Rembrandt, Jacob blessing the sons of Joseph.

Fig. 25. Autun, Bibl. Municipale, ms. 19bis, Sacramentary of Marmoutier.

Fig. 26. Autun, Bibl. Municipale, ms. 19bis, Sacramentary of Marmoutier.

Fig. 27. St. Gilles (Gard), tympanum, Adoration of the Magi.

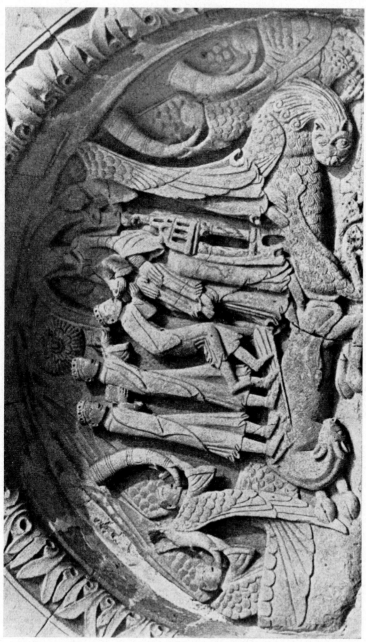

Fig. 27'a. Neuilly-en-Donjon, tympanum, Adoration of the Magi.

Fig. 28. Gerona, Cathedral Treasure, ms. of Beatus on the Apocalypse, f. 257, Daniel.

Fig. 29. Paris, Bibliothèque Nationale, ms. latin 8878, f. 233v, Daniel.

Fig. 30. Naples, Museo Nazionale, Greek vase, Offerings to Dionysus.

Fig. 31. Athens, National Museum, Greek lekythos.

Fig. 32. Athens, National Museum, Greek lekythos, detail.

Fig. 33. Padua, Arena Chapel, fresco, Giotto, Betrayal of Christ.

Fig. 34. Padua, Arena Chapel, fresco, Giotto — Christ and Judas.

Fig. 35. Assisi, San Francesco, fresco, Betrayal of Christ.

# INDEX

illustrations are in italics

deviation from, 19
meaning changed in translation, 19–20, n.22
as precedent for action, 21
prospective interpretation of,
    in commentators, Christian, 17–18, Jewish, 17, n.19
    in Gospels, 18
    in Old Testament, 17
    in Paul, 18
reduction of, in illustration, 10, 11
secularizing interpretation of, 34–35
spiritualizing interpretation of, 16, 18
symbolic sense of, 10, 13, 14
    fourfold interpretation of, 13
    meaning of, changed in illustration, 12, 13, 23, 30
See Meaning, Interpretation of text, Symbol, Old Testament
Thekla, n.35
Theodosian codex (408 A.D.), n.63
Theodosius, Expugnatio Cretae, 21, n.30
Three Boys in the Furnace, n.35
three-quarters view of head, 38, 44, 45, 46, n.91, n.95, n.97
Tikkanen, J. J., n.6, n.43
Titian,
'Schiavone', n.89

Toulouse,
    St. Sernin,
        tympanum sculpture, n.51
Treitinger, O., n.43
Types, n.20
    See Prefiguration

Urban, Pope, 21, n.32, 22
Utrecht University Library Ms. 484 (Psalter), 14, *1*, n.5, n.51

Venice, Bibl. Marciana, Psalter of Basil II, 25, n.44
"Verus Israel", 28
Vieillefond, J. R., n.44
Vienna, Nationalbibliothek, cod. theol. XXXI, Genesis, 28, *15*
Vuillard, E., n.87
    See New York

Wilfrid, bishop of York, 20
William of Auvergne, 35, n.75
Wind, E., n.63
Wolf as symbol, 10, 11
Woodcuts,
    See Bible, printed

Zacharias, Pope, 25, n.47